BE KIND

BE KIND

A TRIBUTE TO
CAROLINE FLACK

EMILY HERBERT

First published in 2020 by Ad Lib Publishers Ltd
15 Church Road
London, SW13 9HE
www.adlibpublishers.com

Text © 2020 Emily Herbert

Paperback ISBN 978-1-913543-95-2
eBook ISBN 978-1-913543-94-5

A CIP catalogue record for this book is available
from the British Library.
Every reasonable effort has been made to trace copyright-
holders of material reproduced in this book, but if any have
been inadvertently overlooked the publishers would be glad to
hear from them.

Printed in the UK
10 9 8 7 6 5 4 3 2 1

CONTENTS

1

STRICTLY CAROLINE

On 20 December 2014, the twelfth series of *Strictly Come Dancing* reached its triumphant finale. A little-known television presenter named Caroline Flack had won. It was a massive triumph, catapulting her into quite another league and setting the scene for a glittering career which would make her a household name, afford her some of the most high-profile roles on television and present her with opportunities afforded only to a few. Caroline was to go on to lead an extraordinarily glamorous life that will remain in the public memory.

And although she already had a substantial amount of television experience before she took to the dancefloor – to say nothing of a private life that had also attracted a certain amount of attention – it really was *Strictly* that started it all. Many felt it was her finest hour and as she became the series winner, she had never looked better or happier. Paired up with the Russian Latin and ballroom dancer Pasha Kovalev, this had been by no means a foregone conclusion: other contestants included Frankie Bridge from The Saturdays, Simon Webbe from Blue, pop star Pixie Lott and Jake Wood from *EastEnders*, who put in a pretty impressive salsa early on. Nor was Caroline an obvious hoofer: to begin with, at least, she came across as faltering and nervous, with a very shaky cha-cha-cha as her debut.

But as the weeks progressed, a change seemed to come over Caroline, with her confidence and ability growing in equal counts. For a start, she was clearly enjoying herself, not always a given in these shows. Secondly, the public loved her. Beautiful, photogenic and sporting a gorgeous array of costumes, Caroline began to show an increased ability, a sense of rhythm and a screen presence that, while it had always been present in her television work, was increasing by the day. There was a nail-biting moment when she once finished in the bottom two, but Caroline rallied like the pro she was.

A rumba, a quickstep and a paso doble all impressed, followed by a jive in Blackpool that really knocked the crowds for six. In an unashamedly high-spirited performance, the couple danced to Elton John's 'Crocodile Rock', Caroline dressed in a Union Jack dress and Pasha as a Buckingham Palace guard, complete with distinctive hat: they scored thirty-seven points that night, to the delight of the crowd. Judge Bruno Tonioli gave her a ten; head judge Len Goodman, giving her nine, said: 'If you are in the dance off this week I'm going to run to the end of the pier and dive off naked.' (He didn't.) 'You can't half flick, Flack.' There was also a nine from Darcey Bussell and another from Craig Revel-Horwood, who commented, 'I thought you executed that with military precision.' Judy Murray was the contestant to leave that week.

Indeed, the audience loved the performance: Caroline's dress was reminiscent of the famous appearance made by

Spice Girl Geri Halliwell at the 1997 Brit awards, clad in a Union Jack miniskirt that she later confessed she'd made from a tea towel and which went on to achieve iconic status. And it was that image that Caroline put on Instagram the year after *Strictly*, when reminiscing about her time on the sequin-heavy show. 'I just loved it,' she later told *You* magazine. 'I loved pretending I was a dancer every day, going to rehearsals in my legwarmers with my coffee in my hand. That was the bit I loved most – the performance days were terrible and nerve-racking, to be honest.' Not that it showed – Caroline was getting so good that there was even speculation about a future role in a musical on the West End stage.

And, despite catching her dress in her heel a couple of times, her confidence continued to grow, culminating in a salsa in the semi-final that produced the top possible score of forty. 'She bangs, she bangs!' screeched Bruno. 'You're a super-charged engine fuelled by sex appeal!' That was followed by another two scores of forty in the final, a cha-cha-cha to 'Can You Feel It' by The Jacksons and a showdance to 'Angels' by Beverley Knight. As if that were not enough, there was yet another forty for a charleston danced to 'Istanbul (Not Constantinople)', originally written by Nat Simon and Jimmy Kennedy, making Caroline the first celebrity contestant to score the maximum forty from the judges in all three of her dances in the final and setting the record for the longest consecutive run of forty marks. And what really came through was how much she clearly enjoyed herself on the show: 'You don't feel bad when you're dancing,' she once said. 'You can't feel unhappy; it's impossible. It's such a natural way to release endorphins.'

It had been quite an experience. There had been four couples in the last show: Mark Wright and Karen Hauer were the first to go out in fourth place; pop star Frankie Bridge and Kevin Clifton and singer-songwriter Simon Webbe and Kristina Rihanoff were the other runners-up. 'There were four Beatles, three musketeers, two Ronnies but only one winner on *Strictly*,' chortled Len, over-egging it a little perhaps, but it summed up the atmosphere that night. Something special had appeared on the screen.

When she won everyone involved sounded nigh-on delirious. The cha-cha-cha to 'Can You Feel It', had an over-excited Bruno shrieking, 'My golden sex goddess!' 'Angels' prompted the audience to spring to their feet, with Darcy exclaiming, 'That was like watching a beautiful contemporary ballet for me, and you'd be in my company any day' (high praise indeed. from a ballerina of her status).

Caroline herself was euphoric: 'This has been the best experience of my whole life, mostly because of Pasha, but also because of the other contestants,' she said in the wake of being named the winner. 'I'm so lucky to get to know this incredible bunch of people.'

The series was considered a triumph, regularly beating *The X Factor* in the ratings and peaking at 11.4 million viewers during the final. It had been a life-changing episode: 'I think all people who've been on *Strictly* like to talk to others who've been on the show and share their experience,' she said afterwards. 'And it's always exactly the same. You go through the same emotions. It never quite leaves you. It's always just here somewhere. It's a real magical thing to have taken part in. It's not so much a job – it's more of an experience.'

Caroline also went on to call winning *Strictly* the biggest achievement of her life, but there was another element at play as well: it was the breakthrough that pushed her into the public's consciousness. She had a solid portfolio of television appearances and a couple of high-profile romances, including two Harrys – Styles and Windsor. But this took her into a different league, that of much-loved national treasure and household name. It was one of the reasons that both grief and disbelief greeted her death less than six years later: how could a beautiful and vivacious woman, with so much going for her, possibly have reached such depths of despair?

But even at the time of her win there were signs that not all was well. For a start, Caroline's personal life was in turmoil. And as she later revealed, she woke up the next day feeling desperately unhappy. 'I couldn't get up and just couldn't pick myself up at all that next year,' she later said. 'I felt ridiculous, being so sad when I'd just won the biggest show on telly. However, I felt like I was being held together by a piece of string which could snap at any time.'

It is easy in the wake of a tragedy to say that people should have spotted sooner what Caroline was going through. Her arrest for the assault on her boyfriend, tennis player Lewis Burton, in December 2019, was the culmination of a tumultuous personal life; the threat of prosecution and losing (if possibly only temporarily) her position as the presenter of *Love Island* weighed far more heavily on her than anyone realised at the time. In retrospect, the fact that she was not allowed to be in touch with Lewis – who did not want the prosecution to go ahead – seems cruel, not least because it deprived her of the support of one of the people she was closest to at the time.

But, as it was widely conceded, Caroline had had problems in the past. And, indeed, she never made any secret of her woes, openly talking about the use of antidepressants and having, as so many women in the public eye do, to put up with violently unpleasant trolling on social media, especially in the wake of the arrest. But at the same time she was an effervescent presence, a bundle of energy that the nation took to their hearts.

It is not uncommon for an animated performer to hide personal pain, but after her death, and in an attempt to provide an explanation for the tragedy, the finger of blame pointed everywhere. Certainly the abuse she had to put up with on social media must have had a devastating effect on a fragile woman and there were immediate and justified calls for social media platforms to exercise more control over what they allowed to remain on their sites. But the plain fact is that nobody could really have predicted what would have happened.

The nation's grief, however, was of a different order from that usually experienced after a sudden and unexpected death. There was shock, of course, that a woman who seemed to have so much to live for could have reached such a state, but even more there was the sense that a personal friend had passed away. Caroline Flack, or Flacky, as she was commonly known to many, was one of a generation of stars who charted their every move on social media, but she did so in a manner that was even more revealing than most. With 2.7 million followers on Instagram and over 3,800 posts, her life was charted in eye-watering detail: innumerable posts charted her trips abroad, her attendance at awards ceremonies, her fashion stylists, her drinking pink champagne and her love of dogs, alongside occasional references to mental health issues and much, much more.

Much of it was indisputably glamorous, featuring exotic locations, designer clothes, celebrity friends and a fast-paced lifestyle, but it strangely both managed to give the illusion that her followers knew her well while at the same time detracting from the truth. In the wake of her death it was commented that she was the poster-girl for a world of reality television stars and life of social media, and this ultimately led to terrible problems. And that certainly had the ring of truth.

Instagram was also the vehicle that was to provide an insight into her suffering in the wake of her death. Her devastated mother Chris released an unseen Instagram post to the family's local paper in Norwich that underlined the true state of her feelings, but which she had been advised not to post: 'For a lot of people, being arrested for common assault is an extreme way to have some sort of spiritual awakening but for me it's become the normal. I've been pressing the snooze button on many stresses in my life – for my whole life. I've accepted shame and toxic opinions on my life for over ten years and yet told myself it's all part of my job. No complaining.

'The problem with brushing things under the carpet is … they are still there and one day someone is going to lift that carpet up and all you are going to feel is shame and embarrassment. On 12 December 2019 I was arrested for common assault on my boyfriend … Within twenty-four hours my whole world and future was swept from under my feet and all the walls that I had taken so long to build around me, collapsed. I am suddenly on a different kind of stage and everyone is watching it happen. I have always taken responsibility for what happened that night. Even on the night. But the truth is … It was an accident.

'I've been having some sort of emotional breakdown for a very long time. But I am *not* a domestic abuser. We had an argument and an accident happened. An accident. The blood that someone *sold* to a newspaper was *my* blood and that was something very sad and very personal. The reason

I am talking today is because my family can't take any more. I've lost my job. My home. My ability to speak. And the truth has been taken out of my hands and used as entertainment. I can't spend every day hidden away being told not to say or speak to anyone.

'I'm so sorry to my family for what I have brought upon them and for what my friends have had to go through. I'm not thinking about how I'm going to get my career back. I'm thinking about how I'm going to get mine and my family's life back.'

It was a way of giving Caroline a voice after her death, something her grieving family clearly wished to do. 'Carrie sent me this message at the end of January but was told not to post it by advisers but she so wanted to have her little voice heard,' Chris said. 'So many untruths were out there but this is how she felt and my family and I would like people to read her own words. Carrie was surrounded by love and friends but this was just too much for her. Her friends Molly, Lou, Sam, Liam and Simon need a very special mention and lots of thanks for trying so hard to keep her safe. Jody, her twin sister, was there her whole life for her but this time nothing could take away the hurt of such injustice. As Carrie would say, "In a nasty world, just be kind." It was describing how she was feeling and what she had gone through – no more than that. It was not blaming anyone or pointing any fingers. We want people to read it and want it to be shared through the EDP [*Eastern Daily Press*] who we really trust and always have done.' Poor Jody was the one who had to identify her sister; a dreadful task for anyone but perhaps even more so for a twin who was still in a state of shock.

Caroline's statement certainly provided an honest assessment of her state of mind and there was unease at the fact that she had been advised not to release it. Despite a huge amount of publicity surrounding mental health issues in recent years, including some valuable work done by members of the royal family, it was telling that Caroline's advisers clearly felt that she would damage herself by admitting to her own fragility. Questions were also raised about the world in which she worked, and above all, *Love Island* itself.

It was a shallow show, based entirely on manipulating the emotions of a group of absurdly attractive individuals and there had been some much-publicised tragedies on the back of it – contestants had taken their own lives. To focus so entirely upon appearance, to create situations in which people were tempted to switch loyalties at the drop of a hat and then to leave the contestants to cope with their own brand of celebrity in the outside world was clearly too much for some. And while Caroline was obviously a presenter of the show rather than a contestant herself, that meant her celebrity was far greater than that of the other people who featured on *Love Island*, with far greater pressures and a need to keep up appearances that would have been too much for many to bear. But it was not *Love Island* that provided the tipping point; it was the night in which everything had got out of control.

Despite intensive criticism from many quarters, the Crown Prosecution Service (CPS) decided to press ahead with the prosecution and it seemed that it was what would be made public that was too much to bear. Caroline was afraid the jury would be shown police footage: 'Her biggest fear was that the body-cam footage would be made public,' said a friend. 'She realised that it was going to be shown in court if it came to court. She felt that, from that moment, her life would be ruined forever. I hear that the footage is quite distressing.' People in a position to know said that it was the shame and embarrassment that had got to poor Caroline. She had been advised not to expose the true state of her mind on Instagram but now she faced not being able to stop the release of footage she had no desire to see being made public.

After she died, those who had been involved with Caroline over the years, both personally and professionally, reacted in shock. 'We are absolutely devastated by the tragic news that Caroline, a much-loved member of our *Love Island* family, has passed away,' said *Love Island* narrator Iain Stirling. 'Caroline and me were together from the very start of *Love Island* and her passion, warmth and infectious enthusiasm were a crucial part of what made the show connect with millions of viewers. Like many of you, right now we're all just trying to come to terms with what's happened. My only hope is that we can all try to be kinder, always show love and listen to one another. Caroline, I want to thank you for all the fun times we had making our favourite show.'

Nor did *Strictly* forget its old friend. 'The entire *Strictly Come Dancing* family are heartbroken to hear this incredibly sad news,' they said in a statement. 'Caroline had an infectious energy and passion for dance, she shone brightly in the *Strictly* ballroom every week and became an incredible champion. Words cannot express our sadness, she was simply one of a kind. We are sending love to all her friends and family during this difficult time.'

In the immediate aftermath of the tragedy, there was of course a backlash among many. *Love Island* came off air for a night and there were calls from various quarters that it should be brought to a permanent end, not least from the parents of contestants who had also committed suicide after appearing on the show. It is impossible to say if there was a connection to Caroline, but in her absence viewing figures had already fallen for the first time since the show was relaunched in 2014, with a million fewer tuning in. Her importance to the success of the show could not be overestimated.

There were also calls for 'Caroline's Law' to stop the media bullying celebrities, although how to define bullying and how far this should go – would publishing the hypocrisies of a politician also be banned? – was impossible to define. The CPS was hauled over the coals, not least because Caroline's boyfriend, Lewis, the person she was charged with attacking, had not wanted the case to go ahead. There was a heated debate in many quarters. The CPS can press ahead with charges even when the victim has withdrawn their complaint in order to protect those who live with violent abusers and are too afraid of possible retribution to press their case. The decision can be taken out of their hands to help them. But did this really apply in this case? Many argued that common sense alone would have established that this was a one-off case involving a vulnerable woman in the public eye. Could not some degree of latitude have been observed?

The CPS was clearly doing its duty and it was not alone in coming under fire in the wake of the tragedy. Journalists were accused of having 'blood on their hands', an accusation that those who knew Caroline well strongly refuted, not least because, unlike many celebrities in her position, she enjoyed spending time with journalists. The coverage in the wake of the arrest had certainly been extensive, but it was sympathetic in parts. There were some ill-advised headlines, but no one had realised the depth of her suffering. Her ex-boyfriend Andrew Brady blamed her management company. Another ex, Danny Cipriani, said that she had called him in the hours before it happened, that 'it was ultimately embarrassment and shame that killed her', and that he was wrestling with his own mental health issues in the wake of her death. The Met referred itself to the police watchdog, the Independent Office for Police Conduct, although it emphasised that this was standard practice in a case of this type and no individual had been suspended or was being held responsible. No one seemed exempt.

There was yet more controversy on the back of the fact that *Love Island* had been running throughout the tragedy, while the contestants, this year based in South Africa for the first-ever winter series, had been as usual isolated from the outside world and were thus totally unaware of what had happened to the woman most closely associated with the show. They were only quietly informed of the tragedy off-screen, right at the end, which cast a certain shadow over proceedings. Paige Turley and Finley Tapp were crowned the winners but the final show in the series was dedicated to Caroline, and a montage of her most memorable moments from 2015–2016 was shown.

Laura Whitmore, a friend of Caroline as well as being Iain Stirling's girlfriend, had been standing in for her in the course of the show and, of course, was as shocked as everyone else. The Irish presenter, thirty-four, had a difficult task to perform, required to be both an entertaining presenter, as well as acknowledging the seriousness of the situation. The common consensus was that she pulled it off quite well. She was clearly emotional as she said, 'The past week has been extremely difficult, coming to terms with the loss of our friend and colleague Caroline. We're thinking of her family and everyone who knew her at this time. Caroline loved *Love Island*, she loved love and that's why tonight's final is dedicated to her.' The montage followed, showing Caroline at her shimmering best: 'Are you ready for love?' she asked a group of contestants. Wide praise for Laura followed on Twitter – where else? – as it was acknowledged she had made the best of a difficult time.

There was a good deal of soul-searching in the wake of all this, from all segments of society and Laura lashed out on Twitter at one paparazzo who had followed her and Iain at the airport in South Africa.

Another ex of Caroline, pop star Harry Styles, performed at the Brits shortly after the death: amid a change of outfits in the course of the evening, there was a small badge attached to his lapel which read, 'Treat people with kindness.' This was a message that was increasingly associated with Caroline, under the phrase, 'Be kind.' It was his first public appearance since the news broke and although he had not said anything, his mother, Anne Twist, tweeted, 'Heartbreaking #ripcarolineflack'. He sang 'Falling' from his album *Fine Line*; many fans were near tears in what was widely considered to be a tribute to Caroline.

Harry also wore a black ribbon during the Brits, held at London's O2 Arena and he was not alone in paying tribute. Presenter Jack Whitehall sent his condolences to her friends and family, saying, 'She was a kind and vibrant person with an infectious sense of fun. She will be sorely missed.' A black-and-white photo of her appeared on the screen as the credits rolled; there was a palpable wish that someone could have done something, alongside a desire to ensure that Caroline would not be forgotten. Nor was she. Her image was everywhere that night.

The truth is that there was no one person, organisation or anything else that was really to blame. A set of circumstances that came together simply sent her over the edge. But the Caroline Flack that should be remembered is a very different one: a pint-sized star, fizzing with energy, ambition and a popular presence on the television screen, someone who created an atmosphere of warmth and liveliness around her. She was much loved.

That is the Caroline who will be remembered: one who brought joy to the nation. This is her story and, the ending apart, it is a joyous one. Caroline achieved a huge amount and she will be remembered for many decades for transforming herself from the girl next door into – well, the girl next door. But the neighbour was the whole nation and the girl next door was the person men wanted to date and women wanted to be. Truly, the nation's sweetheart. And nothing changed that.

2

A STAR IS BORN

It was 9 November 1979. Great Britain had just been through the winter of discontent, with widespread strikes including those by the Transport and General Workers' Union (now Unite), refuse collectors and gravediggers; an attempt by the governing Labour party to cap public-sector pay rises and keep soaring inflation under control, a freezing cold winter, a shambolic atmosphere at 10 Downing Street and finally a vote of no confidence in the government, leading to the general election on 3 May 1979.

No one knew it at the time but it was to be a turning point in the nation's history, as the Conservative party, led by Margaret Thatcher, was pitched into power and began eighteen years of Tory rule, a time that would utterly transform Britain, turning it from the 'sick man of Europe' into an economic powerhouse, brimming with confidence, opportunity and pizzazz. Britain was to change completely in almost every conceivable way and although the advent of reality television, social media and near instant stardom, the milieu in which Caroline was to spend most of her adult life, was still decades away, there was change in the air.

Ambition was no longer looked on as something to be ashamed of, there were opportunities in the pipeline that no one could previously have dreamed of and there were chances for women to make a life that did not just revolve around marriage and children. Margaret Thatcher, who was both married and had children, was the living embodiment of that: she had made it to the highest position in the land; she was the leader of the country and for her to do that showed that anything was possible for a truly determined woman. Caroline would follow a very different path, but she grew up knowing that hard work and putting the hours in paid off. Maggie had done it and look what happened to her. And at the same time the very nature of television was changing.

In 1979 there were only three channels: BBC One, BBC Two and ITV and while it is often now thought of as the golden age of television, with families gathering round the screen to watch one programme together and then talking about it to colleagues at work the next day, to modern eyes the era appears impossibly dated. Many people still watched in black-and-white and the box in the corner from those days now looks like something that belongs in a museum. By 1990, when Mrs Thatcher stepped down, televisions had become sleeker and more stations, including Channel 4 and Sky One had started to appear. The medium, along with the bigger society beyond it, was changing.

But in 1979, the dawn of a new era, all that was still to come. And so that was the backdrop into which Caroline Louise Flack was born that day, 9 November, the youngest of four children who included her twin sister Jody. She had popped out six minutes before Caroline. Jody was the sibling with whom, although they took very different paths,

Caroline maintained a lifelong closeness and devotion of the type that perhaps only twins can understand. She was often asked about it but how could she know what it was like to be a twin, Caroline later commented, when she had never known anything else? Initially, it was Jody who was set to be called Caroline. But at the last minute their mother Chris decided that Caroline didn't suit her. And so the young star in the making got her name.

Theirs was a conventional family set-up. Caroline's father, Ian, was a sales representative for Coca-Cola; her mother was Christine, née Callis and the family – at the time the twins were born – lived in Enfield, north London. And although they moved out of the city when Caroline was still a baby, that geographical location began a lifelong love of Tottenham Hotspur. The Flacks had a slightly bigger family than was usual in the days of the nuclear set-up and it was to remain at the very core of Caroline's life: the oldest of the children was Elizabeth, then ten, and brother Paul who was eight when she and Jody arrived.

After her father landed a job in management, the family moved to Great Hockham, in Thetford, Norfolk, which Caroline herself dubbed, 'the middle of nowhere'. It was a picture-postcard village, centred round a village green, with a primary school and a pub. The family home stood in a 1970s' cul-de-sac surrounded by woods and trees. Caroline would talk about its isolation, and how the local children would speak of witches and the ghosts in abandoned local villages. Norfolk can be very remote and this patch certainly fitted that description. She had a quiet, rural upbringing, a world away from the bright lights that would one day make up Caroline's world. The children would play in the village and the nearby countryside, Jody and Caroline inseparable, not least as they were much younger than their older siblings. Outside, as the 1980s gathered pace, momentous global events unfurled. There was the Falklands War, the miners' strike and the rise of the yuppie. The Soviet Union began to totter. The whole world began to change.

Opportunities were opening up and the previously hidebound structure of Britain was shifting. Caroline's father went on to run a clothing manufacturer and her mother worked for a local newspaper. Yet, while everyone was doing well, Caroline later recalled a working-class childhood in which money was tight, at the beginning, at least. On one occasion she needed pink tights for ballet lessons, for example, but had to make do with white ones dyed pink with Ribena. That detail was telling. Dance, it seems, had been a feature of her life from the very earliest days. So, more problematically, was eczema. All little girls are aware of their appearance from a very young age and Caroline, ironically for someone who was to grow into being a beauty, was very aware of hers. She was a mass of insecurities right from the start and her skin condition no doubt contributed to that.

But it would be very wrong to portray her childhood as an unhappy one: while there were downsides, there were huge positives, not least because she was brought up by parents who adored her and made the family the centre of all their lives. And she was fortunate enough to have loving siblings, too. The closeness with her twin Jody dates back to those early days: the two shared a bed until they were four and they were in the same class at school together. In her autobiography Caroline would relate that having a twin meant she never felt alone and never experienced loneliness in those early years. Natural playmates, although not identical, the children were unaware of quite how much was shifting beyond the boundaries of their home. But it would come to affect them soon enough.

Ian did well in his new career and, when Caroline and Jody were seven, the family moved again, now to a bigger house in East Wretham, which Caroline said was even more remote than the home they had lived in before. About six miles away from Thetford and twenty-five miles from Norwich, the small community had St Ethelbert's parish church, set in the traditional Norfolk stone, a pub and an old RAF site that was used for British army training. Nearby, the ruins of the fourteenth-century church of St Lawrence provided the local beauty spot, looking grand against the goings-on of the little Norfolk village. It may have been remote, but it was an ideal place to house a young family.

'We had a pond and a climbing frame, as well as the chickens and a rabbit called Boris, because our big sister was in love with Boris Becker,' Caroline recalled in her autobiography *Storm in a C Cup*. Boris presumably lived in a hutch outside. The family couldn't have actual pets in the house because of Caroline's eczema. She also had to avoid foods such as nectarines, apples and cherries, all of which could bring on an attack, the first of a surprisingly high number of problems Caroline had to deal with when she was very young. Many believe these issues contributed to her insecurities in later days.

In many ways, however, it was a rural idyll and, although Caroline's sights were soon to be set on a larger stage, for now she was content to spend time taking walks in Thetford forest with her father and sister, collecting tadpoles, as so many small children do and 'making her own entertainment' as the family lived a long way out. They would listen to the radio and sing along, giving Caroline, perhaps, her first taste of the performing urge that would come to dominate her life. Television – still with limited choice – played a part, of course, but the children remained unaware of the seismic changes taking place in the wider world. Entertainment was changing, too: while there was still no reality television as such, there were talent shows. Admittedly these were not new, but the idea of a television presenter becoming a big star in his or her own right was growing. And in March 1985, a soap opera launched in Australia, called *Neighbours*. Still running to this day, it would be screened all over the world. It, too, would have an impact on Caroline, who went on as a young girl to idolise one of its stars.

Caroline attended a small village primary school called Great Hockham, set between Thetford and Watton, with four classes for children aged three to eleven. It had a lot of involvement with the local community. She then went on to Wayland high school, Watton (also the alma mater of cricketer Shaun Bailey), which originally opened in 1926 and fifty years later became one of only six schools in Norfolk to go comprehensive, another of the seismic changes to be seen in the UK during the 1970s. (It is now an academy.) Caroline enjoyed dancing lessons in the school and appeared in village pantomimes and plays, as well as joining the school's dance group, The Gug. Right from the start it was clear where her interests lay.

But as previously mentioned even back then there were signs of great insecurity, which stemmed from … who knows what? Caroline and Jody were not identical twins and friends say that Caroline thought that Jody was both prettier and cleverer. Her eczema made her hate her skin and she so loathed her 'skinny' legs that she would wear five pairs of tights to make them seem more substantial. But given the closeness between the two sisters, her sense that her sister was superior didn't involve sibling rivalry, but rather Caroline's good heartedness in assuming someone else, in this case her twin sister, was bound to hold the upper hand. This tendency to put herself down persisted: she went on to develop a veneer, an outer confidence that did not reveal the inner trauma from which she was suffering. It went back to earliest childhood and there were problematic episodes, of which more anon.

She also thought that Jody was the more talented of the two. But again, this did not give rise to any rivalry – quite the opposite – and the two seemed to grow even closer as the years wore on, with the adult Caroline often releasing pictures of the pair on Instagram, some dating back to early childhood. The twins often had their arms curled around one another, a charming picture of inseparable sisters who never grew apart. But there were some differences: 'My twin Jo and I also kept diaries when we were growing up,' Caroline told the *Mail On Sunday*. 'We would go into each other's rooms and see what we had written – we couldn't be more different. Jo's would say, "We had pie for dinner," and mine would say, "I hate Mum"!'

But while there was closeness within the family home, there were problems outside it, of the type that can blight a life. Caroline was bullied, which can leave a person with a lifetime of insecurities that can never really be overcome, especially if they are already self-conscious about their appearance. Apart from the eczema, Caroline was also extremely thin and hated it at the time – ironic, given that so many young girls can develop serious eating disorders in striving to lose weight. 'I was underweight, so I'd be back and forth to the doctors to get weighed,' she told *Cosmopolitan*. 'I also suffered from bad skin, allergies. Then I went off food and just didn't want to eat ... I didn't like being small. I was picked on and I was the only girl who wore trousers at school. I was really paranoid about my legs.'

Her legs would become celebrated when she was older and this sort of outcome was not uncommon. Many of the world's acknowledged beauties are told that they are too thin or too tall or too unusual when they are growing up, the very qualities that lead to their later success, but devastating to have to listen to as a child. Caroline also, unaccountably, hated her arms and, as an adult, while she because famous for flaunting her legs in very short shorts, her arms frequently remained covered up.

There were other issues, as well, which certainly weren't enough to scar her for life, but which provided jolts that would go on to cast a shadow over her. When she was just six Caroline fell into a swimming pool wearing a rubber ring that turned upside down. Mercifully, her father noticed her legs were in the air, powered over and saved her, but the episode left Caroline with a lifelong fear of the water and did nothing to provide her with calmness of mind.

Right from the start she was into singing and dancing. 'I was always putting on performances for my family, probably much to their annoyance,' she recalled in the wake of winning *Strictly*. 'I was very young when I realised this is what I wanted to do – probably from the moment I could speak. I remember the village hall where I grew up put on a pantomime every year and when I was seven I got a part. That only helped to convince me that this is what I wanted to do for the rest of my life – not to be the back end of a donkey, I should add, but to be in this industry.' Of course, the industry that she yearned to be a part of and which she was obsessed with from early childhood was one that focused very heavily upon appearance. And Caroline would never be entirely happy with hers.

Body image is one of the great concerns these days among young girls (ironically, reality television is said to enhance the problem) and as a young girl's body begins to grow and change, so there is all the more opportunity for angst. This was certainly the case with Caroline. Yet more childhood insecurities were revealed when Caroline later contributed to a book called *The Booby Trap and Other Bits and Boobs*, put together by Caroline's friend Dawn O'Porter and which was set to benefit a breast cancer charity when it came out in 2013. Perhaps unsurprisingly it involved another of the great female obsessions – breasts. An awful lot of young girls on the verge of puberty suffer all manner of agony in thinking theirs were misshapen and Caroline was no exception to that.

'When I was growing up I only had one boob,' she confided, talking about her breasts' comparative sizes and shapes. 'It was fairly disturbing as I was the only one who knew, and I used to stuff the other side of my bra with tissue. It wasn't until one day when it just got too lopsided that I ran down to the kitchen where my mum was making carbonara and shouted out in despair, "I've only got one boob." Mum sat me down and told me it was totally normal. Weirdly, within a couple of months, I grew a second boob and all was OK. You can rest assured now that I have two fully functioning boobs!' She was making a joke of it, of course, but for a child growing into adulthood it was not funny. All these little masses of insecurities could not have helped her, then or as an adult and, while Caroline asserted it was a funny story, it clearly left its mark.

There was one terrible incident in Caroline's childhood that she never forgot. When she was just thirteen her friend

Johanna Young, a year older, went missing just before Christmas in 1992, and was later found murdered. The killer was never found. It was a particularly shocking event in such a small and isolated community and, unsurprisingly, caused terror among her own friends, all of whom were convinced the same thing would happen to them.

'She [Johanna] was last seen walking off towards the High Street at about half past seven,' Caroline recounted in her autobiography. 'They didn't realise she was missing until the next morning, Christmas Eve. Her body wasn't found until three days later, half-naked, in a flooded clay pit down a track not even a mile away. I started not going out after dusk, convinced I was going to be murdered, convinced the murderer was somewhere around … just waiting.' She described the school bus passing Johanna's house as it made its way towards the school gates and worse still, seeing Johanna's Christmas presents piled up in the window. A hush would fall on the bus as it made its way on.

While she might not have been aware of the great changes taking place across the globe, Caroline was very up to the mark on television and show business and was beginning to have an inkling as to where her future might lie. Britain was fairly obsessed with *Neighbours* in the 1980s and 1990s and she was one of its most avid viewers from the moment it launched in the UK in October 1986, becoming even more successful in this country than it had been in its native Australia. And Caroline had dreams, even as a small child. Her great heroine was Kylie Minogue – to whom she bears a slight resemblance, not least as both are tiny – who played the tomboyish mechanic Charlene Robinson and whose onscreen relationship with Scott Robinson, played by Jason Donovan, was mirrored by their real-life relationship off screen.

Caroline increasingly set her sights on a career in musical theatre, although typically she downplayed her talents in later life: 'I've always felt the need to overcompensate but I know my limits,' she once said. 'My first ambition was musical theatre but I realised quite early on that I wouldn't make the grade.' That *Strictly* experience suggests otherwise, as indeed does the fact that she actually did end up in several stage shows, but by now Caroline was following her own path, like her hero Kylie Minogue, who by the end of the 1980s was moving from being a soap star to becoming a successful singer. She was reinventing herself. Taking a lead from her heroine, Caroline decided to follow her own dreams and despite repeatedly putting herself and her abilities down, was good enough to land a place at the Bodywork Company in Cambridge at just sixteen. She thus left home for what would turn out to be for good, with a whole new life ahead of her, and she was determined to put this opportunity to good use. School was now behind her and it was time for the next phase.

The Bodywork Company, founded in 1981 by Theresa and Patrick Kerr, is an establishment that trains dance professionals and, early in the 1990s, introduced a three-year diploma course in dance and musical theatre. Nestled in the heart of the stunning university town of Cambridge, the school was close to the famous medieval college of King's Parade and The Backs, the beautiful college grounds that run down towards the River Cam. In the spring, ranked series of undergraduates, clad in full robes, could be seen parading towards the Senate House to receive their degrees.

Redolent of tradition, but with a thriving student scene that centres not just around the university, but the numerous other educational organisations that have sprung up in the town, the streets of Cambridge are thronged with 'town and gown', the student population that flock there in term time and the local population who are resident all year round. Bitterly cold in the winter, amid the flat, East-Anglian countryside, and packed with tourists in the summer, Cambridge might have been more famous for its ancient university than its dance academy, but it was an idyllic place for Caroline to spend three years learning her trade.

And the academy was an excellent one, too, with numerous students ending up in West End shows such as *42nd Street*, *Cats*, *Fame: the Musical* and *Five Guys Named Moe*, to name but a few. Caroline learned how to dance professionally as well as being taught every aspect of entertainment: how to comport herself, make her presence felt, command the stage and to present herself to her very best advantage. This training was to be invaluable when she started her career and indeed, although it took a while for her to reach the very top levels of public consciousness, it did not take her long to get started.

And she was to end up in musical theatre, her great dream as a child, for short stints, for all that she never lost the knack of putting herself down. In later years she would put photographs on Instagram of that time, showing a nascent performer brimming with energy, vigour and ambition. She looked stunning, too. No one would ever be able to explain why a woman as beautiful as Caroline would have such insecurities about her looks: those razor-sharp cheekbones that played so well on television, were apparent back then, as well as a beaming smile that would not have looked out of place in any West End theatre. Young as she was, Caroline was on her way.

The only downside was that for the first time in her life, Caroline was living apart from her twin sister Jody and, although the two remained as close as ever, they did not see one another with the same frequency. Caroline found this difficult. And, while Jody had also been part of the amateur theatricals when both were younger, it was now clear that she was going to have a very different life from her twin. Caroline described them as being the opposites in terms of personality, but that the two sides of them made a whole. For now, however, the twins had to accept that their lives were to take very different paths. Jody must have been thrilled for her sister, who was now getting closer to the dreams that she had held throughout her life.

Self-deprecating she might have been, but Caroline was capable of very hard work. The school was at the centre of Caroline's life for the next few years and she threw herself in to it, not only on the dance side, but learning the basics of singing and acting, too. She made quite an impression, both on her teachers and fellow students, who would remember her very fondly. There was no side to her and no arrogance – quite the opposite – just a determination to succeed. And she stayed in touch with her teachers afterwards, who were thrilled as they saw her rising up the ranks of the showbiz world.

'She was very, very hard-working; even then we knew that she would go somewhere,' founder Theresa Kerr later told ITV Anglia. 'She was ambitious but not in a way that took anything away from her – she just worked hard. The thing people don't realise is, although she became famous as a TV presenter, she was actually a "triple threat" – someone who is good at singing, dancing and acting. She was a great singer as well as a great dancer. It was really nice that she actually got to do a West End show. When we did a twenty-fifth anniversary gala she compered that show for us – she was great, she was famous then and didn't have to do it.' Generous to a fault, it was hardly surprising that Caroline was so popular among those she knew.

In fact, Caroline shared a flat back then with Theresa's daughter, so the school founder was able to see her in both professional and domestic circumstances. Like so many performers, it was clear that Caroline was at her happiest when she actually had to perform. 'Obviously she was happy,' Theresa told *Good Morning Britain*. 'She was very happy on stage. Her comfort zone was in performance. She was always going to climb to the heights.'

Others also remembered that she stood out, even in those early years when she was still learning her trade. At the time that Caroline joined *Strictly*, it was not yet well-known that she had trained as a dancer, but the *Daily Mail* managed to track down the mother of another student who had been training at the same time. Karen Laogun's son was Jay Banks and she said, 'She was a great dancer, even back then. She did loads of dance, jazz, the lot. She did a degree and I watched the show for her leaving graduation. I would say she was probably the best in the class, she was really talented.' It was a view widely shared elsewhere.

She was very popular with other students, displaying that girl-next-door quality that she maintained throughout her life and which was another of the keys to her success. Caroline had that rare combination: she was beautiful, but she was also relatable, with no airs and graces and the ability to get on with anyone. Despite having to put up with broadsides from some quarters over various difficult episodes in her life, there wasn't a bad word about her from people who actually knew her, whether personally or professionally. That was the same when she was at Bodyworks: she was very widely liked.

She was determined to make it in show business, that most tricky of professions. Bernadette Battom, two years Caroline's senior, was another student at the school and also a flatmate, the two sharing a place with three other performers. She revealed that even back then Caroline was unlike so many students who treat further education as one long party and who stay up all night and skip classes. Caroline was extremely determined and knew just what she wanted right from the start.

'She was so full of happiness, energy and drive,' she told the *Sunday People*. 'She was a bundle of confidence and always got picked for everything. We were working so hard, we were coming home exhausted, so we didn't go out loads or party. Caroline knew where she wanted to go and she was focused on that. She wasn't the tidiest housemate but she was very popular. People were drawn to her.' She went on to recount how Caroline's laughter would fill the house: she took her studies seriously, but was always laughing, joking and making light of her life. She was clearly happy: despite the pain of being apart from Jody, she went on to call her time at Bodyworks 'the best years of my life'. She was young, she had it all before her. And her infectious personality was making her friends, as it was to do throughout the rest of her life.

People continued to be drawn to her; while she lost touch with some of her fellow students over the years, she remained in touch with Theresa and the school and would go back to visit them. As her career progressed, she became an inspiration for many of the school's future students: if she could do it, then perhaps they could do it.

In 1999 Caroline graduated, taking part in a final-year show and, while she did not go straight into musical theatre as she had previously dreamed of doing, she did step in to a phenomenally successful career.

And Caroline was still just nineteen. Her years of living on her own might have been difficult at times but it had taught her independence; she was still close to her family and, above all, to Jody and remained so for the rest of her life. But she was ready to venture out on to a wider stage now, one for which in many ways she had been preparing since early childhood. What would she go for? Would it be acting, singing or dancing? The answer was: a little bit of all of them although, of course, it was as a presenter that she would come to be best known. A brilliant future awaited her, one in which she and one of her early inspirations, Kylie Minogue, would meet and become friends. Kylie by this time had become a bone fide superstar and Caroline was still impressed by her, although her hero-worship had become something more akin to one professional admiring another.

Now, in whatever field it turned out to be, Caroline was determined to become what she had always dreamed of being. A star.

3

BABY STEPS

Caroline Louise Flack was out on the scene. A new graduate after her three years in Cambridge, with a diploma in dance and musical theatre, she had her heart set on becoming a West End star, an ambition she was to achieve – but not yet.

Instead, a couple of years were spent finding her feet, joining a dance troupe and – following the grand old tradition of resting actors – making ends meet with jobs including a stint in a pork factory, of all the unlikely employment. 'I loved it,' she told the *Daily Mail* in 2007, just as she was beginning to edge into public awareness. 'In the end I had to give it up because no one wanted to come near me because I reeked of pork.' She was practical: she had to earn a living and, if she hadn't yet landed a leading role in the West End, then other employment would have to do. Other casual jobs were to follow.

Caroline had moved to London, almost an imperative for anyone looking to make it in show business, and started establishing herself slowly, seeking out professional breaks, getting to know the capital and establishing herself on the scene. Caroline would never have any problem making friends and she did so now, meeting other young hopefuls, attending auditions and tackling her new life with characteristic humour and determination. It is said that when a newcomer arrives in London, they tend to stay in the area in which they first settle and that was the case with Caroline. She settled in north London, which was home to among others the raucous 'Primrose Hill set' – including Rhys Ifans, Ewan McGregor, Sienna Miller and Patsy Kensit – and it was there that she stayed for the rest of her life.

There was a breakthrough of sorts in 2001 when Caroline made a blink-and-you'll-miss-it appearance in a racy, made-for-TV film about the lives of holiday reps in Ibiza. Called *Is Harry on the Boat?*, it gave rise to a television series, which featured no one from the film and ran for two series. In the film itself, Caroline's character was actually known as Blonde. For a film that few people have heard of, it featured a surprisingly high number of unknowns who were to go on to become household names: apart from Caroline herself, it included Danny Dyer, Davinia Taylor, Will Mellor, Ralf Little and John Simm.

It was work. But her first real break came the following year on the show *Bo' Selecta!*, which ran on Channel 4 between 2002–2004 and on which she was to appear a number of times, as well as making a lifelong friend of its creator. Billed as an adult sketch show, *Bo' Selecta!* was created by Leigh Francis and employed surreal, sometimes somewhat smutty humour, while giving the impression of allowing anarchy to reign. The idea behind it was that the central character was a stalker played by Leigh himself called Avid Merrion, who was clearly unhinged, and who spent his time tracking down celebrities, also portrayed by Leigh, using latex facemasks. The title was based on a line from the song 'Re-Rewind' by the Artful Dodger and Craig David (of whom more below) 'The crowd say bo selecta' was a lyric from the song.

The celebrities themselves who were being lampooned were some of the biggest names in show business and some (although not all) were flattered by their portrayal in the show. They included Elton John, shown as an angry, aggressive and antisocial character; illusionist David Blaine; Kelly Osbourne, originally placid in her onscreen persona, but then ranting at the camera; Michael Jackson, a mental patient who swears constantly and has verbal tics; Mel B, who unsurprisingly comes across as something of a professional northerner and, in latex mask form is seen as trying to seduce Patsy Kensit; and Craig David himself. Leigh also played 'the bear', a perverted teddy bear who meets celebrity guests – real ones, not those portrayed by latex masks – and gets them to read a bedtime story. The story would usually end up with the bear becoming sexually aroused. The mixture of pastiche celebrities and real celebrities might have been unusual, but they made for interesting viewing and the show itself became something of a cult.

Not that everyone was won over. Craig David, by some accounts, was not entirely happy with his portrayal as an arrogant Yorkshireman with a plastic peregrine falcon named Kes (a reference to the 1969 film). He did, however, actually appear on the show himself. He later said he regretted it although he then retracted the regretting and said that he didn't mind really and that he had been advised to express regret. Somehow it all fitted in with the onscreen uproar. Craig was a recurring presence on the show with catchphrases including, 'Proper bo I tell thee' and 'Can I get a reeewind?' The show was sometimes criticised as being a little juvenile, as it undoubtedly was, but was very popular in its day and spawned two successful Christmas singles, 'Proper Crimbo' and the double A-side 'I Got You Babe'/'Soda Pop'.

The series, still available on DVD and on Channel 4's website, kicked off with Avid Merrion showing viewers around his flat before heading off in search of his first celebrity obsession, Davina McCall. In the second episode celebrity pastiches include Britney Spears, Enrique Iglesias, Gareth Gates, Elton John, Tess Daly and Penny Smith. It also featured Michael Jackson and his pet monkey Bubbles engaging in a blind boxing match.

By this stage in Jackson's life, the endearing child star who had made it into adult fame had long been replaced by a desperately eccentric character, clearly damaged beyond repair by a traumatic childhood from which he would never recover. He was unrecognisable from his younger self. And Bubbles was part of that: back in the day, the real Bubbles was a very well-known figure in his own right: Jackson bought the chimp from a Texas research facility in 1988 and took him on tour: Jackson and Bubbles would wear matching outfits and the chimpanzee also lived at Neverland Ranch. He slept in a crib in Michael's bedroom, used Michael's toilet and ate candy in the Neverland cinema. While this might have seemed charming in some ways, given that Michael appeared to be investing his emotions in a monkey rather than a genuine human being, there was something desperately unhealthy about it. Ultimately, it was tragic, for both man and chimp, but inevitably, there were a fair few people who could not resist the opportunity to make a joke.

By the time Leigh got around to his take on events, both Jackson and his pet had been well and truly mocked across the board. It had been the appearance of Bubbles on the scene that was said by some to have been the first indication of quite what a peculiar and strange personality Jackson had become. In the event, by 2005, Bubbles had become an aggressive chimpanzee, unsuitable as a companion for a human and was sent to a Californian animal trainer. He ended up in the Center for Great Apes in Wauchula, Florida, where he lives to this day.

But Leigh's take on it was rather different. In his portrayal, Bubbles is played by none other than Caroline herself. Michael shows viewers around the home he shares with his siblings Janet, Tito and Jermaine and, of course, Bubbles. The footage gained a new generation of viewers when Caroline's appearance in *Love Island* made her a household name, generating much amusement (and the observation that, although she looked a little different, she had not seemed to have aged in the intervening years). In the world of *Bo Selecta!*, it turns out that Bubbles is not a monkey at all but Jackson's assistant. 'You didn't think Bubbles was a monkey, did you?' asks Jackson/Leigh. 'Sure, she eat my banana, but she don't have an inch of hair on her goddamn body. You know what I'm saying?' He continues to Caroline, who is behind him, singing into a microphone: 'Bubbles! What did I tell you about using my equipment?'

'Michael, I was just doing my track,' says Bubbles, before storming out of the studio.

'Just get your white ass out of here. Shamon! I don't want no one touching my s**t,' 'Michael' replies. Leigh, dressed in a bright-orange leather ensemble, a reference to Michael's most famous video, 'Thriller', looked nothing at all like Michael, but that was part of the point. No one was actually supposed to look like the people they were portraying on the show.

It was all pretty silly stuff and fairly harmless. Caroline was to appear on the show five times in total and formed a lasting friendship with Leigh and the woman who would become his wife, who was also Caroline's make-up artist. Leigh went on to form another comic alter ego, Keith Lemon, who would present *Celebrity Juice*, on which Caroline would also appear – of which, more anon. And they were far more than just colleagues on the show. Caroline credited Leigh with having a huge effect on her career, not just in giving her a breakthrough, but in teaching her some of the skills she would go on to use in her later work. 'I hadn't done any presenting work before I met Leigh Francis and so the avenue to the TV presenting world was opened up by him,' she told the *Independent* in a series called 'My Mentor', after the event.

'We first met around four years ago and he was dressed as Craig David in an office reception. I thought he was a complete loon. I really tried to talk to him normally but he would not come out of character. Leigh is so spontaneous. I had a part as Bubbles in *Bo' Selecta!* and I always wanted to work with a script but he taught me how to work without one. He also taught me how to be myself and relax more in front of the camera.'

It was the start of a solidly respectable television career. There was to be no great leap forward just yet, but in essence Caroline was putting in the hours, learning her trade and also settling down in her new home, London. Regular contact was maintained with her family and she remained close with all of them, especially Jody.

As the twins progressed into their twenties, the divide in the paths their lives were taking became ever more obvious: Jody worked as a film editor for a little while, but met her partner when she was still very young and went on to have three children with him, Zuzu, Willow and Delilah. She largely shunned the limelight and while, like her more famous sister, she was an avid user of social media, she did not reveal much about her private life. Caroline adored being an aunt and, as she herself would put it, the twins lived their very different lives through each other, vicariously.

The work continued to come in – until the very end of her life it never stopped. From the outside at least, her life could scarcely have looked more glamorous. From 2003 Caroline put in a stint on *The International Pepsi Chart Show*, a re-edited version of Britain's *CD:UK*, interviewing major names in the pop world, including the Red Hot Chili Peppers on their European tour. The programme had started as a networked UK radio show in 1993 before being taken up by Channel 5; it was lively, personality-led, hosted big prize competitions and shared the official Top 10 countdown with BBC Radio 1. Caroline was the international presenter for several editions, including Norway and Tahiti. It was her introduction to the world of the very famous and she was particularly impressed by the Chilies.

'For my first ever job on TV, I had to hang out backstage at one of their gigs,' she told the *Daily Mail* in 2007. 'I hadn't ever interviewed anyone before. I went backstage with my little camera and met [lead singer] Anthony Kiedis. He's a bit of a womaniser and, frankly, the sexiest man I've ever spoken to. He turned me to putty.' But was it really rock'n'roll? 'I didn't find any drugs backstage with the Chili Peppers,' Caroline continued. 'In fact, they really weren't very wild back there at all. No groupies or anything. They have this canteen where they all hang out and eat posh dinners.'

Her sense of humour was clearly still intact. And her personal style was beginning to develop. Like a number of women who turn into beauties, somewhat to their own surprise, Caroline was beginning to realise that while she might have been down about her appearance, the rest of the world most certainly was not. Those skinny legs had turned into very shapely pins and Caroline began to show them off with a series of hot pants, and this would become her standard look over time. Her hair periodically changed colour throughout her life, but at this point she was mainly blonde. She might have worried about her eczema, but no one else did, and being small was another advantage because she was extremely photogenic. It is said the camera adds ten pounds and so she was better off at that size. Caroline had that mysterious quality that cannot be defined, that makes some people blossom when a lens is upon them. Her former teacher Theresa had said that she came most alive when she was onstage and the same thing happened when the cameras started to roll: Caroline was a complete natural and this was apparent right from the start.

At the same time, Caroline was building up a circle of friends, acquaintances and settling into her new life. It was not all work: there was a fair bit of play as well. The 'Cool Britannia' period that had characterised the late 1990s was over but a new decade had begun and a fair bit of what was happening was centred on the part of London that Caroline had made her home. A close friend ran the famous Hawley Arms in Camden, north London, which became a magnet for the in-crowd, including Liam Gallagher, Kate Moss and Pete Doherty. It was the favoured local of Amy Winehouse, who would go onto be another young victim of celebrity culture. She was then at the height of her fame and frequently stalked by the paparazzi. She was notorious for hopping behind the bar and serving the punters. 'She used to come in and say: "Craig, babydoll, can I serve some drinks?"' the Hawley's manager, Craig Seymour, told *Vice*. 'I've seen grown men break down in tears after being served by Amy.'

The MTV studio was nearby, which partly explained the clientele, including Tim Burgess of The Charlatans: 'Britpop had The Good Mixer but The Hawley Arms was the follow-up to whatever the follow-up was – a scene so cool it didn't have a name,' he told *Vice*. 'The Hawley Arms was the who's who of what's what. Amy Winehouse was pulling pints when I first went in – pretty sure she didn't work there, but it was that kind of place.' In other words, it was indie central, and Caroline was getting used to rubbing shoulders with the celebrity crowd, along with owners Ruth Mottram and Doug Charles-Ridler, who had bought the pub in 2002, the year Caroline began to establish herself, and transformed it by installing a jukebox and hosting the odd gig by locals. Previously there had been no live music in the place. On Caroline's birthday, people ended up dancing on the bar; it was in many ways the perfect way to live her twenties. Caroline had money coming in, because she was earning regularly, but she also still had the freedom that would be lost when fame made its mark on her scene. Unlike Amy, at that stage Caroline could do pretty much what she wanted without exciting comment. It was to be some years before her every move aroused the interest of the paparazzi and social media.

The scene couldn't last. Poor Amy died a few years later at just twenty-seven, a victim of her own success and demons that could not be kept under control. Everyone else dispersed and the pub was at one stage threatened with closure, although it managed to stagger on in the end. These days The Hawley Arms is better known as a gastropub than anything else, and indeed it almost vanished altogether after a fire – Caroline attended the fundraiser to save it.

Another favourite hangout was The Lock Tavern, also in Camden, and a pretty trendy place in its own right. Known as a rave pub after it opened in 2005, it was famous for its live gigs and club nights. It too still exists and continues to hold live gigs, and has also more recently become well-known for the food. Russell Brand was at that time cutting a swathe through the female population of London (and beyond) and he and Caroline went on a date around this time. Nothing came of it romantically but the two were to remain firm friends, with Russell penning a powerful message about her after the tragedy occurred.

Like so many in her role, Caroline found that she was mixing with the same people both personally and professionally. She began presenting the links between videos on the E4 Music strand – E4 being a part of Channel 4 – which ran throughout much of the day following E4's relaunch as a freeview station in 2004. The people who appeared on the show may well have been relaxing afterwards at The Hawley Arms. Another gig on E4 was *The Games: Live at the Trackside* with Justin Lee Collins. This was a reality sports game in which ten celebrities competed against one another in sports such as weight-lifting, diving and gymnastics. Originally presented by Jamie Theakston, aided by Jayne Middlemiss providing trackside reports, Caroline and Justin took over for series three and four. While a lot of Caroline's work by this time involved glamorous international travel, much of the filming for this show took place in and around Sheffield, that fine English city providing the Sheffield Arena, Don Valley Stadium and Ponds Forge.

Caroline was getting increasingly busy: her portfolio included a regular segment on the video games show *When Games Attack*: this ran from 2004–2005, presented by

Dominik Diamond and filmed in different locations around the UK rather than in a studio, and frequently involving saucy jokes. Caroline had a segment called 'Flack Attacks', which involved her travelling around Japan, looking at the weird and wonderful elements of that country, such as giant robots, cosplay and anime. There was more than one bizarre moment, including having a robot fall in love with her, as Caroline related to the *Daily Mail*.

'Apparently, he's the first robot ever to have feelings,' she recalled, 'and his eyes turned to little hearts when he saw me. It wasn't the dullest date I've been on. They're about a million years ahead of us in Japan – they even have dog translators out there. When your puppy barks, this box tells you what he's saying. Though it's always something like, "I'm hungry", or, "Stroke me, you b*****d."' Caroline was also a frequent commentator on cultural differences between east and west: when at a cosplay convention, seeing a queue of middle-aged men waiting to have their picture taken with a young girl in costume, she commented that that kind of behavior in the UK might well have resulted in arrests.

While not quite well-known enough to get mobbed on the street, Caroline's somewhat wild lifestyle, full of parties and men, had attracted enough attention for some hilarity when her next gig turned out to be as a presenter on children's TV. She had been appearing in the papers fairly regularly by this stage and was savvy enough to know that this was all to the good: if you want a successful career as a television presenter, then it's crucial people should take an interest in you. Not that her new role should have been the cause for laughter: for a start, quite a few children's TV presenters had somewhat racy lives (sometimes exposed in the most unfortunate way) and anyway, her animated, girl-next-door persona made her perfect for the role. In 2006 she began a two-year role as a presenter on *Sam & Mark's TMi Friday* – TMi for 'Too Much information', with Sam Nixon and Mark Rhodes. The show was broadcast on BBC Two and the CBBC kids' channel. A lot of very successful television presenters start on children's TV: Caroline didn't actually start there, but learning to cope amid the chaos of sticky-back plastic and primary colours means you can deal with almost anything. And she did.

Replacing *Dick & Dom in Da Bungalow*, Sam and Mark were a pair of former *Pop Idol* contestants, and the show was the standard mix of games, cartoons, competitions, celebrity guests and music videos. The first series, in 2006, had a reality element to it, a first for a children's television show, in that Sam and Mark lived in the 'TMi flat' throughout the week in the run-up to the show, preparing for the big broadcast, although this was dropped by the time of the second series. In the first series they would have a segment called, 'Surely They Can't Make a Game Out of This', in which the two men were given a number of implements and told to use them to make a competition for studio contestants. The episodes would finish with a Chinese challenge, in which one of the presenters was given a task to complete in nearby Chinatown. Caroline, who came across as a mixture of glamour puss, helpful assistant and big sister, left after the end of the third series, although viewers did not learn this until the beginning of the fourth. There was no mystery to her departure – she was simply becoming too busy elsewhere to carry on and, indeed, many of her current gigs were now overlapping.

In fact, children's television suited the wackier side of Caroline's personality: she was always up for a laugh and these were the ideal circumstances in which to allow those instincts full reign. Dressing up as something outlandish? No problem. 'I've got a full-size banana outfit, which is good fun, too,' she told the *Daily Mail*. 'The great thing with kids' TV is that you can come up with any stupid idea and nobody will care, they'll just give you money. I say, "I want to dress as a banana," and nobody asks why; they just go off to the tailors and make it happen.' And they did.

By now she was really spreading her wings. She added a new music show into her repertoire, which in some ways was a welcome contrast to the antics on *TMi*. It also reflected her real interests: there wasn't a lot of sticky-back plastic at The Hawley Arms. 'I'm starting a new show now called *Live At IndigO2*, which is quite different to what I've done before because everything I've done before is quite comedy-based and light-hearted,' Caroline told the *Independent*. 'On the other programme that I present, *TMi*, I've dressed up like a bear, done an angry dance and asked people what their favourite ice cream is. On this show I'm interviewing people like Paul Weller, who don't want to be asked what their favourite ice cream is.'

It was a weekly helping of live music from an intimate London venue, the little sister of the O2 near Canary Wharf in east London, the whole site once being the Millennium Dome. The programme went out late on ITV2 and featured many musicians, including the kind of indie performers that Caroline was hanging out with in real life. Three bands would perform live sets in front of the audience; they were to include The Charlatans, The Zutons and The Feeling.

'The show's been absolutely brilliant so far,' Caroline told the *Manchester Evening News* shortly after the programme began to air. 'We've filmed two episodes so far – one with Paul Weller, The Courteeners and Scouting For Girls, and another with One Night Only, Amy Macdonald and The Enemy. We have people coming along to a gig, the band play eight or nine songs and we film it. That's it. We'll never say, "We need to film that again," or, "Can the crowd clap now, please?" It's genuine reaction to what the guys are doing on stage … I'm really looking forward to The Fratellis and We Are Scientists. They're supposed to be a good laugh so I can't wait to meet them.' But could they live up to Paul Weller? 'He was absolutely amazing and really went for it,' said Caroline who, despite the fact that she now mixed in these circles, had lost none of the tendency to be a little star-struck on occasion. 'I didn't get to interview him, but we did have a good chat by the side of the stage.'

The show did present challenges, though, in showing three live performances by different artists and series producer Jim Parsons commissioned sound recording company Red TX to make sure it all ran smoothly. The idea was that it should give the feel of being at a live gig. 'Normally we link up to the house PA system at the venue for our broadcast splits, but one or two of the bands brought in external systems that gave us some interesting interface issues to deal with,' said Red TX director Conrad Fletcher. 'However, we quickly managed to iron those out. We're recording each band live and in stereo and backing up to multi-track. There is time for a quick remix if it's needed but so far none of the bands has requested this.' It was not one of her most high-profile gigs, but it did extend Caroline's experience.

Work and play were running hand-in-hand at this point, as they were to do in many ways throughout Caroline's life. When attractive young people work and play in the same places, it is no surprise that romance is often on the cards. And, indeed, indie rock bands began to play a role in Caroline's personal life by 2007, when she dated Dave Healy, aka Dave Danger, drummer in The Holloways. It was a serious relationship, which was to last for three years. The Holloways were an English four-piece rock band from north London, Caroline's milieu, and they enjoyed a fair amount of success before they split in 2011, including making it to Glastonbury. Dave went on to perform with the Burning Beaches. He and Caroline were pictured about town together, attending gigs and showing up at all the most fashionable venues. But their relationship was not to stay the distance.

Caroline did not cope well with the break-up; she lost a great deal of weight and that concerning emotional fragility reappeared. It was and remains a mystery why such an attractive and lively woman who was, after all, going to present one of the most famous dating shows on television, found it so difficult to build a relationship of her own. But after three years, the couple called it a day.

Caroline was to be comforted by a very regal suitor indeed, of which more in the next chapter. But while her love life might have been faltering, her career most certainly was not. Next up was another children's television show, *Escape From Scorpion Island*, which Caroline presented with Reggie Yates. The idea was that the contestants, children aged between eleven and fourteen years old, would 'escape from an exotic island with a mind of its own'. When the ten contestants arrived on location in Fernando de Noronha, Brazil, they were divided into teams of five each, called Sting and Claw. Over the next three weeks they had to complete various challenges, the last one being an escape from the island. The finale took place on Shadow Mountain.

The critics seemed a little bemused, with one comparing it to *Lord Of The Flies* and another asking whether it should be classified as an interactive educational experience or *I'm A Celebrity* ... for children, but it did well enough, with Caroline staying on to host a second series. International travel was by now becoming an even bigger part of her regime as well.

But Caroline was enjoying her professional life and building up relationships, not just with fellow celebs, but also journalists, to whom she was always drawn. Many found her far more open than most celebrities, almost too open sometimes when she revealed the full extent of her insecurities, but that vulnerability was part of her appeal. Her life might have been glamorous, but she was not so very far removed from the lives of the viewers. And most of the time it seemed to be working out for her. But there was much more in the pipeline, both romantically and on the professional front. There was all to play for – and she did.

4

HARRY WHO?

There is a long tradition of mutual attraction between royalty and showbiz: there was even a film made about it in 1957, *The Prince and the Showgirl*, starring Laurence Olivier and Marilyn Monroe. The phenomenon has been known to spill in to real life, too, with the actress Grace Kelly becoming Princess of Monaco.

And, indeed, it should be no surprise that there is a mutual interest: power in a man and beauty in a woman both exercise a strong attraction and princes tend to be powerful (or, at least, come from families that are influential) and actresses/TV presenters are almost always extremely good-looking. And there are other crossovers: monarchs and their kin do have a certain kind of celebrity, even if it's different to that of a TV presenter. Both are accustomed to being in the limelight. So, it should have been no surprise when Caroline caught the eye of her very own prince, the Duke of Sussex – Prince Harry.

In 2009, when Caroline and Harry were first introduced by TV and radio broadcaster Natalie Pinkham, both were still reeling from break-ups. Caroline had been extremely cut up over the split from Dave, while Harry wasn't having much luck in his own love life. He had finally split from his long-term girlfriend, the Zimbabwean businesswoman and lawyer Chelsy Davy, reportedly because she could not cope with life in the spotlight. The couple had become the subject of intense speculation and couldn't move without making the front pages; Chelsy finally decided she'd had enough.

This was not to be the only time Harry split up with a girlfriend because she just couldn't stand the incessant attention. He went on to decide that he actively wanted a woman who was in the public eye because she'd be able to cope with the constant interest of the media and, indeed, he went on to marry the actress Meghan Markle. Ironically, they were later both to decide they couldn't put up with constant harassment from journalists. But back in 2009, that was all to come and, after meeting the bubbly and effervescent Caroline, the two became an item for a brief time. They had a lot in common: both were lively, bright and chatty. Both were extremely popular with the public. Both thoroughly enjoyed having a good time. And on top of that, of course, was good old physical attraction: both were young and gorgeous and they had that inexplicable element: chemistry. In short: they clicked.

In her autobiography, Caroline described how Harry arrived in the company of a couple of friends and soon the two were chatting and laughing and they became a pair. Rumours leaked out that they were seeing one another and at first the public was not sure whether to believe it. Harry and Caroline? Could the stories possibly be true? But true they were and, in many ways, in retrospect, why not? Both were young, single and bubbly; Caroline was a couple of years older than Harry, who was still serving in the army and was then twenty-five. The age gap was not so great as to make a difference (and certainly not so much as in the case of the second Harry in her life) and both were looking for love. At that time Harry seemed to have a specific type – petite and blonde – and Caroline conformed to that too.

And the public goodwill towards both of them was palpable, although there was also a certain amount of shock expressed in some corners. Prince Harry had been the nation's darling ever since he was a little boy and especially after he lost his mother in such tragic circumstances; Caroline was by now well-known enough to have prompted a considerable fondness from the public, with a palpable hope invested in her that she would find Mr – or perhaps Prince – Right. Could this be the one? Alas, no.

Somewhat ironically, again, as with Harry's previous relationship, it was the publicity that made it impossible. Sightings of the couple had resulted in a great deal of news coverage, with the result that attention was diverted from Caroline's independent life and career. 'Girl from Norfolk (the county of Sandringham, the Queen's country home) who had worked in a pork factory, no less, was dating a prince of the realm!' was the gist of it all. Caroline put it succinctly in her autobiography: she went from being Caroline Flack, television presenter, she said, to 'Prince Harry's bit of rough'.

In later years, Caroline was to clam up sharply on the subject of Harry. When giving interviews for her book, she made the point that she was not talking about the relationship per se, but the effect the publicity had on her friends and her family, which was considerable. No details of their time together were forthcoming and, as time wore on, she refused to talk about the fact that the relationship had happened at all. All she would confirm was that both Harrys in her life had known she was going to write about them – and, which was quite true, she never said anything about either that could have caused embarrassment or hurt. Her life more usually consisted of wearing her heart on her sleeve, but on this occasion she was not prepared to do so. Asked once on television whether, had there not been so much publicity about it, her relationship with Prince Harry could have gone the distance, even there she refused to say a word. It was quite admirable of her to be a public figure who could have commanded millions had she gone into detail but to choose not to do so. It may be the honourable thing to do, but it is not always as easy as it looks.

But did she actually need the money now? Almost certainly not. Caroline was perhaps being overly harsh on herself in referring to herself as 'Harry's bit of rough' but that public perception was enough to draw matters to a close. And the very fact that the pair had garnered so much attention was another sign that Caroline's career was soaring and that an awful lot of people knew who she was: two years previously she had hosted *Comic Relief Does Fame Academy* and, when a presenter becomes involved in Comic Relief it is a sure sign they have become one of broadcasting's favoured stars. If there is one biennial event in the show business calendar that is sacrosanct, it is Comic Relief's Red Nose Day: a chance for the great and the good to pay their dues to society, by helping the less fortunate. It had been running since 1985 and anybody who is anybody appears at it in some guise at some point.

And there were lots of different ways to take part, too. Comic Relief had massively outgrown its beginnings and now existed in all sorts of different shapes and forms. *Comic Relief Does Fame Academy* was launched in 2003, a spin-off of the original *Fame Academy* show, in which celebrity students of the academy would sing. The finale of the show was broadcast on Red Nose Day itself on BBC One, BBC Three, BBC Prime and the CBBC channel – namely, all the outlets that were becoming very familiar to Caroline by then. In total it was to air three times: 2003, 2005 and, finally, 2007, which was when Caroline became involved. Her work with the programme made the point that she was increasingly becoming part of the celebrity establishment herself now.

The show took place during the two weeks leading up to the nationwide fund raising efforts and cheerful stunts of Comic Relief and Red Nose Day itself: the students would perform a song of their choice, under guidance from the husband-and-wife vocal coaches Carrie and David Grant, with the footage going out live. Judges would comment on their performance, after which voting lines would open for two hours, with the stars departing as the show continued. In the results show, three performers were kept to the very end, each required to sing their song again, with a process of elimination involving students and judges leading to the final winner being picked. Patrick Kielty was the presenter throughout for BBC One, aided first by Cat Deeley and then by Claudia Winkelman; Caroline covered the proceedings for CBBC, the children's channel for which she had done so much in the past. The winner of the first series, which featured nine celebrities, was Will Mellor, another of the alumni from *Is Harry on the Boat?* A lot of performers from that long-forgotten film were, it seemed, doing pretty well for themselves now.

And none more so than Caroline. The likes of John Simm might have become serious actors – in fact, it was around that time that he was having massive and well-deserved success with the superb time-travelling police show *Life On Mars* – but the bouncy and bubbly television presenter was having the time of her life. The third series took place in *Fame Academy*'s new home, the debating chamber in County Hall, on the south bank of the Thames, right in the capital's heart. It launched on 3 March and ran until 16 March, which was Red Nose Day itself. In her role, Caroline was replacing Sophie McDonnell (who herself had replaced Holly Willoughby) in presenting with Jake Humphrey, another CBBC regular. Caroline, Sophie, Holly and many others, including Davina McCall, Claudia Winkleman, Tess Daly and more; they were all part of a generation of lively, feisty television presenters and often ended up substituting for each other or appearing on each other's shows.

Preparations wore on. The Grants were back, as was Richard Park, who was the head teacher and judge. He was joined on the panel by soprano Lesley Garrett and Craig Revel Horwood, always adept at producing publicity for anything he appeared on. The celebrity line-up included Rowland Rivron, Miranda Hart, Linda Robson and Tim Vine, but the winner that year was the socialite Tara Palmer-Tomkinson, yet another who was fated to die young. Tara was to pass away in 2017 at the age of forty-five of a perforated ulcer, much to the shock of the nation. But back then, a decade previously, Tara, whose family were close friends with Prince Charles (the father of Prince Harry; but if Tara and Caroline exchanged a few Windsor insights they didn't tell anyone) was the show's undisputed star. Tara, in fact, was often unfairly depicted as a bit of an airhead, much like Caroline would be on occasion. Somewhat troubled herself, she was a gifted pianist with far more accomplishments to her name than many realised.

The show was a success. And Caroline was attracting even more attention and, the following year, made another leap towards the limelight when she was picked to comment on the semi-finals of the Eurovision Song Contest in 2008 with the broadcaster Paddy O'Connell, a regular since 2004. Getting this gig was another sure sign that Caroline was very much a presenter in good standing with the BBC, although in this case it was BBC Three. You don't get much bigger than Eurovision, even if this part of it was not being shown on one of the mainstream channels. The competition excited affection and derision in equal comment and it was still one of the major broadcasting events of the year. Terry Wogan provided his inimitable commentary in the final and, for the English-speaking audiences, at least, he was still the undisputed star. Sadly, it was to be his last year.

Caroline and Paddy O'Connell were presenting from Belgrade and there were to be nineteen countries competing in what were, for the first time ever, two semi-finals. The hopefuls had been whittled down from forty-three initial entrants, representing the highest number of contestants to start the competition. Eurovision itself issued a press release, introducing Caroline to other countries who did not know her as yet: 'The United Kingdom will, as previously announced, broadcast both semi-finals. Since 2004 we have heard Paddy O'Connell commentate on behalf of the United Kingdom in the semi-finals and last year he was joined by Sarah Cawood as his co-host. This year it has been announced that Caroline Flack will take the place of Sarah. The television presenter, Caroline Flack, is known in the United Kingdom for hosting many well-known television shows such as *The Games Trackside, TMi, Comic Relief does Fame*

Academy for CBBC, etc. and will, as of June, be the host of *Big Brother's Little Brother* on Channel 4.'

Caroline acquitted herself with her usual professionalism, but admitted not every viewer warmed to her earthy style: one viewer emailed to criticise, of all things, her laugh. 'It's a cackle – a dirty, mucky laugh and I love it,' was her defence of her chortle to hot-tuna.com a couple of years later. 'Eurovision's great – it's cheesy and terrible, and that's why it's fun. But after Eurovision I had an email from a bloke who said: "Thanks, you ruined my weekend with your annoying laugh."' But it didn't matter to most who tuned in. In the event, Russia won, with 'Believe' performed by Dima Bilan.

Fortunately, that view of Caroline's laugh was to do her no harm, and her career rollercoaster sped on, with Caroline rumoured to be replacing Dermot O'Leary, as Eurovision's PR department had hinted, on *Big Brother's Little Brother*. *Big Brother* was another of the huge behemoths of British television, even bigger than *Love Island* in its time. Running on Channel 4 for a decade from 2000 before moving to Channel 5, it was based on a Dutch reality television series that had begun in 1997 and was franchised all over the world. Taking its name from the authoritarian powers depicted in George Orwell's *1984*, the shadowy state apparatus that kept a constant watch on absolutely everyone in the book, the premise was that contestants, known as housemates, were kept in a custom-built living area, cut off from the outside world. Each week one of the housemates was evicted following a public vote, with the last one to remain going off with a cash prize. For the full length of its tenure on Channel 4, it was presented by Davina McCall, part of Caroline's ubiquitous girl-gang of television presenters, although she chose not to follow it to Channel 5. And throughout it was narrated by the actor Marcus Bentley, a publicity-shy voice who rarely gave interviews or talked in public, but who managed to end up on one of the biggest programmes on British TV.

From the moment it began broadcasting, *Big Brother* was become something of a national obsession, with numerous spin-offs, including *Celebrity Big Brother* and other non-competitive versions of the show, running not just in the UK but all over the world. Over the course of its run, which finally ended in 2018, there were a total of forty-five series of *Big Brother* in the UK, including nineteen regular series, twenty-two celebrity series and four other series. It was to make stars of members of the public: builder Craig Phillips was the first winner, after sixty-four days in the house; he endeared himself to the viewers by donating his £70,000 prize money to his friend Joanne Harris, who had Down syndrome, and went on to forge a fairly successful career for himself in television, including appearing on *Bo' Selecta!*, as well as in the music business.

There were many others who became famous for riding its coat-tails: Jade Goody, another who died tragically young (aged twenty-seven in her case, of cancer), Alison Hammond, Brian Dowling and Aisleyne Horgan-Wallace, to name but a few. Chanelle Hayes, who appeared in the eighth series, did so well that she ended up with a reality TV series of her own. There were many spoofs and parodies based on the show, including those done by Alan Carr, Caroline's old mucker Justin Lee Collins and Ricky Gervais and it was referenced in many other programmes, including *Doctor Who* and *Extras*.

The similarities with *Love Island* are obvious and, looking back, it is almost possible to say that Caroline was able to use it as something of a dummy run, as it were, for her later and more famous role. Numerous spin-off shows emerged:

Big Brother Eviction, *Big Brother's Bit on the Side*, *Live From The House* and *OK! TV: When 'Bruv Takes Over* were just some. And then we come, of course, to *Big Brother's Little Brother*, which launched in 2001 and ran until the show switched channels; it ran in conjunction with the main series and was presented by Dermot O'Leary from its inception until 2008. It looked at *Big Brother*-related activities outside the house, featuring interviews with celebrities, journalists and housemates who had been evicted, as well as announcing news, updates and who was up for eviction. When Dermot moved on, he was actually replaced by George Lamb, but the fact that Caroline had been in the picture at all showed quite how high her standing had risen.

She ended up working on *Big Brother's Big Mouth*, launched during *Big Brother* six and hosted by another old mate, Russell Brand. It was initially broadcast at 7.30 p.m. on E4 before being moved to a position immediately after the Channel 4 highlights show. It featured a studio audience of fans of the show and two celebrity guests who would discuss the goings-on, while viewers could send in phone messages, texts and emails. In 2007, Russell left and was replaced by a series of guest presenters, including James Corden and Mathew Horne, Davina McCall, Jack Whitehall and, for week five of the 2008 series, Caroline herself. She made quite an impact: Rob Leigh was a *Big Brother* blogger on mirror.co.uk. 'If nothing else, check out this week's host Caroline Flack,' he advised. 'Sheer loveliness aside, her sharp delivery makes her the best presenter they've had on this series.' In the end, that was the full extent of Caroline's involvement, but it clearly showed that she was ready for her next presenting role.

Before ending up with the show that she would make her own, Caroline became involved with some of the biggest names in television. Towards the end of 2008, it emerged that the next of these was to be *Gladiators*, taking over from Kirsty Gallacher later that year. *Gladiators*, an adaptation of a US programme, had originally run from 1992 to 2000 on ITV but was revived by Sky 1 between 2008 and 2009. Ian Wright and Kirsty Gallacher hosted the first series, with Caroline and Ian appearing on the second. It was another programme that was suited to Caroline's lively personality and was to prove a great hit with the viewers; by this time she was well-known enough for news about her to prompt comment on social media and all the coverage was positive.

The series featured thirty-two contenders, sixteen men and sixteen women, who competed in separate tournaments against the gladiators. The aim was to earn as many points as possible before the final eliminator round; the gladiators themselves were for the most part not the athletes who appeared in the first run of the programme, but they did share names with their predecessors (Amazon, Panther, Siren and Warrior) and with those who featured in other international series. Eyebrows were raised over their costumes, which were far skimpier than they had been the first time around – and that was the men. Caroline would later be exposed to a good deal of physical perfection on *Love Island* and, given the amount of oiled and glistening biceps she was now confronted with on *Gladiators*, at least she would then not be seeing anything she hadn't seen before.

One Gladiator, Wolf (aka Michael Van Wijk), had been on the show the first time around and he now featured in series two, when Caroline was the host. The run kicked off in December 2008 with a 'legends special' and six other gladiators: Cyclone (returning from series one), Siren, Amazon, Warrior, Goliath and Doom. The event pool was to feature three new games: 'pursuit', 'suspension bridge' (played over water in the ITV version of the show) and 'rocket-ball', a modified version of swingshot from the original series, in which the players occupied platforms and tried to grab coloured balls.

The original referee had been John Anderson and, following his retirement, boxing referee John Coyle took over. There was a revised element for the eliminator, with a floor travelator introduced as an obstacle before the monkey bars. Like so many of these long-running shows, constant innovation and re-interpretation was needed to keep the viewers' attention and interest and, in the longer term, this second run of *Gladiators* was not to match the first.

The female gladiators comprised of Amazon, Battleaxe, Cyclone, Enigma, Inferno, Panther, Siren and Tempest and the men were Atlas, Doom, Goliath, Oblivion, Predator, Spartan, Tornado and Warrior. Ice and Destroyer, from the first series, didn't return. There were six initial heats, three quarter-finals, two semi-finals and a final that was won by Kathryn Evans and David Staff. There were also five specials, starting with *The Legends Strike Back*, in which original gladiators Lightning, Wolf, Scorpio, Trojan, Rocket, Cobra, Siren and Bullit returned to compete – and lose – against the new gladiators. The specials were to add a separate element to the concept, involving all sorts of permutations of those who were involved and this proved to be a popular part of the show.

This was followed by *Battle Of The Forces*, in which contenders from the RAF, navy and army competed with the gladiators. The female winner came from the RAF and the male from the army. This was followed by *Champion Of Champions*, in which the previous year's winners, Anna and

Simon, competed against Kathryn and David: – Anna and David were the winners. *Battle Of The Athletes* featured four Olympic athletes appearing for charity (boxer James DeGale made the news by being the first contestant to slip on the new floor travellator) and, finally, there was *The Legends' Last Stand*. This was the last-ever episode of the programme and it aired on 25 October, with ex-gladiators Trojan, Ace, Khan, Cobra, Rebel, Vogue, Panther and Siren returning to the arena for one last gasp of glory. They took on the new gladiators. Features included Khan facing Goliath on an event called 'duel', and Wolf battling Trojan on 'earthquake' and, in all, it was a fitting finale to the show. That was to be the end of *Gladiators* for now, at least – there may yet be a future revival – but it had been a good run.

Caroline sparkled throughout. Her lively style, ability to think on her feet and complete grasp of the niceties of this kind of television made her perfect for the role and it put her in yet another high-profile position. Personally, it was at around this time that she had her brief romance with Prince Harry. They were seen together at a Fulham nightclub, which they left together at 4 a.m. and were driven to the royal residence of Clarence House, on The Mall, by a bodyguard.

'It isn't surprising to see them together as they have a lot of mutual friends and are out on the same social scene when Harry is in London,' a friend told the *Daily Mail*. 'Harry thinks she is cute and the feeling is mutual.' Harry might also have appreciated the strength and endurance that was a feature of *Gladiators* – after all, it did feature the armed forces, of which he was a part as a serving army officer.

And after another night at another bar, there was another report: 'They were having a great time and you could hear music, laughter and the clinking of glasses coming from within,' an onlooker told the *Mail*. 'Harry and Caroline were clearly getting along very well, they were laughing and joking and their body language showed they were relaxed in each other's company.' There had been speculation that Harry would get back with Chelsy Davy, but that was looking increasingly unlikely and indeed, she had been linked to the twenty-eight-year old cricket captain of South Africa, Graeme Smith.

Caroline was anything but a bit of rough, but perhaps her involvement with the television show and its format of one-on-one combat made some people believe that she was, in fact, a gladiator herself, rather than just the presenter of the show. But whatever the reasons for the end of the affair in reality, the brief romance did even more to lift her profile and, for ever afterwards, Caroline was to be referred to in lists of Prince Harry's ex-girlfriends. The man himself went on to form a relationship with Cressida Bonas, an actress from a very distinguished family. Later still, by the time Harry married Meghan Markle, his relationship with Caroline well in the past, she still came up in talk about his private life. This included discussion of the list of exes who were invited to the prince's wedding in 2018. Caroline, by then very busy with *Love Island*, was not there.

The relationship with Harry had not been sufficiently serious to plunge Caroline into the black moods she experienced following her previous relationship breakdown and, in any case, if work was the cure for a broken heart, there was still to be plenty of that. In July 2009, she briefly stepped into the role of presenter on *Something For The Weekend*, a Sunday morning show on BBC Two. It took the form of a relaxed chat show format, involving celebrity interviews, based around the preparation of food.

Originally presented by Amanda Hamilton – Caroline stood in for her when she was on maternity leave – Tim Lovejoy and Simon Rimmer, the programme always ran along the same lines: Rimmer (assisted by either Hamilton, Lovejoy, and subsequently guest presenters including Louise Redknapp) would prepare a three-course meal as well as a 'lazy brunch' dish. At the end of the show this would all be eaten.

There were guest interviews; clips from television programmes; a 'deja view' segment featuring an old programme: presenters and guests had to guess the year it was first broadcast; a drinks segment with mixologists (Andy Pearson and Wayne Collins were regulars in the role at a time when 'mixology' was extremely fashionable) and a gadget round-up feature called 'some things for the weekend'. The title of the show was, of course, a saucy reference to the way in which barbers, having shaved and tended their gentlemen, would ask, 'Anything for the weekend, sir?' By which they meant a condom, rather than a three-course lunch, but it all added to the light-hearted appeal of the show. The presenters and guests wrapped up at a round table at which each had a dish that had been cooked earlier. During the meal Lovejoy asked the guests questions posed by the public via text and email.

'I start in July and I can't wait to get cracking,' an excited Caroline told the *Sun* just before her stint began. 'I'm not sure if my cooking is up to scratch but I get on really well with Tim. It will be very different to presenting *Gladiators*.' By this stage she could claim to having presented just about everything from sport to music to celebrity interviews. Whether it was by accident or design, Caroline had also managed not to get herself pigeonholed, which meant that she was a potential go-to pretty much across the board. Whatever the nature of the programme, Caroline could clearly handle it. She was without a doubt one of television's growing stars.

Despite being popular with the public, *Something For The Weekend* was dropped in March 2012 due to budget cuts in daytime programming, although an almost identical programme with the same production team, Lovejoy and Rimmer, named *Sunday Brunch*, soon turned up on Channel 4. Caroline's involvement in the programme had come shortly after the split with Prince Harry and there were remarks from some quarters to the effect that dating a prince had done Caroline's career prospects no harm. This was pretty unfair as Caroline had been building up her career for years before she met the royal, yet she also had to put up with headlines involving the two of them getting 'flack' (geddit) for the relationship. But Caroline took it on the chin.

In her personal life she was next, very briefly, linked with James Corden, who had also just had a break-up – from his long-term girlfriend Sheridan Smith – after bumping in to him at a bar: 'James was stuck to her side all night,' a somewhat breathless source told the *Sun*. 'They clearly had a cracking chemistry and were loving each other's company. James was heartbroken when things came to an end with Sheridan, but he has taken it as a chance to enjoy being single and famous. After a few drinks, James's unmistakable cackle was echoing around the boozer. He was making her laugh and they ended up snogging in the corner of a private room.' Nothing more came of the pairing but it cheered them both up.

But ever more was awaiting Caroline, both in terms of her professional life and her personal one, with another Harry waiting in the wings. Caroline continued to bubble and to sparkle, while maintaining complete professionalism. She admitted that those wild nights at The Hadley Arms meant that sometimes she could be a little bleary in the mornings, but it did not come across on screen. She was a national favourite, a leggy girl next door who had found TV stardom. And there was much, much more to come for the petite bombshell in the years ahead.

5

I'M A CELEBRITY!

Caroline was a celebrity now, no doubt about it. And the prestigious shows were piling up, these stalwarts of British television programming, making an appearance on Caroline's CV. As previously stated, she had shown that she could turn her hand to pretty much anything, and so she did: she was becoming one of a band of go-to girls where television programming was concerned. And so, it was inevitable that her name could crop up in conjunction with one of the biggest televisual names of the lot.

I'm a Celebrity … Get Me Out of Here! was and remains one of the most successful shows on British television. First broadcast on ITV in 2002, it was a show that placed a number of celebrities in the deepest bush somewhere in Australia (initially the location was King Ranch near Tully, Queensland and later Springbrook National Park was used, close to Murwillumbah, New South Wales) and forced them to go through unspeakable ordeals in the form of the 'bushtucker trials'. These were challenges to complete in order to receive food and treats: the public were tasked with phoning in to nominate the celeb to do the task and frequently seemed to take an almost sadistic delight in nominating the person who feared the trial most. Anyone who had previously confessed to a fear of heights would thus find themselves confronted with an abyss beneath them. Those who didn't like water would be plunged into a lake. And so on.

Presiding over all this were Anthony McPartlin and Declan Donnelly, aka Ant and Dec, except for the one series when, due to issues in his personal life, Ant's role was taken over by another television go-to girl, Holly Willoughby. (She was, in turn, to interview Caroline on *This Morning* about her autobiography. And Caroline's name had also come up as Ant's possible replacement. It was a small world.) Ant and Dec were without any doubt the most successful television presenters of their generation: starting out as child actors in *Byker Grove*, where they first met, they had morphed into a hugely popular presenting team, with a chemistry both on- and off-screen.

Their friendship was famous and, while they had not exactly changed the nature of popular television as such, they were hugely in demand, fronting everything from *Ant & Dec's Saturday Night Takeaway* to *Britain's Got Talent*, *Pop Idol* and much, much more. While their presence could not guarantee a show would work, it certainly increased the chances for success, and their air of somewhat teenage affability was exactly right for a programme that, let's face it, contained a certain element of sadism. It boiled down to forcing famous people into doing very unpleasant things. And right from the start, the show was a massive ratings success.

Like *Big Brother* before it, *Celebrity* spawned any number of offshoot programmes, including *I'm A Celebrity: Extra Camp*. This was originally known as *I'm a Celebrity … Get Me Out of Here! NOW!* and was broadcast on ITV2 and UTV, featuring behind-the-scenes footage and interviews with contestants who had already left the jungle. It was initially hosted by Irish broadcaster Louise Loughman, before Mark Durden-Smith and the ubiquitous Tara Palmer-Tomkinson (who herself had been on the main show as a contestant and had managed to make it to runner-up), took over for the next two series. They then gave way to a series of new presenters, including Matt Brown, Brendon Burns, Kelly Osbourne and Jeff Brazier (another one-time reality contestant who was the father of Jade Goody's two children – it really was a small world), and which in turn gave rise to another short-lived offshoot, *I'm a Celebrity … Get Me Out of Here! Exclusive*, which only ran for one series.

I'm A Celebrity: Extra Camp itself had a very respectable run, having changed its name in 2015 and lasted until 2019. It remained popular, but was axed because of high running costs. The programme attracted a rolling caravan of ubiquitous television presenters of which Caroline was now a part. It was in 2009, during the ninth series, that Caroline was added to the roster and she reappeared in series ten (reportedly beating Dec's then girlfriend Georgie Thompson to the role), with roving reporter Joe Swash, who had previously been a contestant on the show himself, reporter Russell Kane and an ever-changing line-up of celebrity pundits.

Getting this show was a big coup for her. 'I have been a huge fan of *I'm A Celebrity* … since it began and I'm really looking forward to presenting the ITV2 show,' she excitedly told the *Sun*. 'It's always been my favourite reality programme and I can't wait to get all the gossip out of this year's celebrities when they come out of the jungle.'

As for Joe, he would also play a big role: 'Joe will be running around doing things like trying out the bushtucker trials ahead of the stars,' a source on the show told the *Sun*. 'The idea is to use his enthusiasm to give the show some extra energy.'

Joe was certainly looking forward to it: 'I'd go back in there tomorrow if they asked me to. Seriously, I loved it,' he told the *Mirror*. 'I'm probably going to get a bit jealous of them. If I could join them, I would. But you know, I get to stay in a nice hotel this time, so it's all cool. Will I feel guilty about the contestants when I'm lording it up at my nice hotel? Not. One. Bit. I've earned it. Having said that, it'll be really nice go back and see the camp from a different perspective. It'll bring back all the memories.' But the show was going to be hard work, too. Although it was filmed in Australia, it went out on primetime UK TV, which meant that many of the people involved had to get used to a very peculiar change in the times they worked. 'I want to get out and be a tourist while I'm over there, but my working hours are quite long,' Joe continued. 'I'll have to do 3 a.m. to midday, daily. So just working out when I'm going to get some sleep will be the main thing. But apparently the jet lag helps loads. You can keep those odd hours if you don't try to adjust to Aussie time. If you stay on British time, you'll feel fine. That's my new saying.' And what about the woman herself? 'I've met Caroline before and she's a lovely, beautiful girl,' said Joe. 'She's going to be superb. I'm really pleased to be doing it with her as she's energetic and she's a real tomboy too, so she's perfect for the role.'

Caroline was looking forward to the gig and with her profile as high as it was, she could well have been one of the contestants herself. For her, as with many others, the role of host or contestant was equally on offer. This idea, however, decidedly did not appeal, with her confessing that even the deprivations involved in going to a music festival had been too much. 'I went to Glastonbury and it was incredibly muddy,' she told the *Daily Star*. She had gone with the man she was dating at the time. 'My fella said he'd never heard anyone moan as much as me. He gave me ten moans, and if I moaned ten times he was going to leave me on my own.' Nor was she mad keen on the creatures in the jungle. She had initially been under the impression she'd be presenting from London, as had been the case for some segments of the show and had been taken aback to discover she was going to Australia herself. In fact, so concerned was she about what she'd find out there – namely, huge spiders – that she'd had hypnotherapy to help her cope. 'I can't bear them,' she said. 'The hypnosis is meant to get me over my fear.' Caroline had a very comfortable lifestyle now and the thought of living rough did not appeal.

But the proceedings soon began, with the assorted contestants heading for the jungle and whatever trials were to be presented to them. Caroline's crop of celebrities included the handsome American actor George Hamilton, aka 'Gorgeous George'; chef and television presenter Gino D'Acampo; former *EastEnders* actress Lucy Benjamin and the interior design couple Colin McAllister and Justin Ryan. *How Clean is Your House?* star Kim Woodburn was in the jungle, too, as was glamour model Katie Price – better known as Jordan – who was the first contestant ever to return to the jungle, having been there five years previously. It was then that she had met and subsequently married and divorced the singer Peter Andre. She was also being paid £400,000, which made her the highest-paid contestant until she was overtaken by the boxer Amir Khan in series seventeen. The professional snooker player Jimmy White, *Hollyoaks* actor

Stuart Manning, Mis-Teeq singer Sabrina Washington and heavyweight boxer Joe Bugner were also there. Alongside them were model and singer Sam Fox, an icon of the 1980s – and in some ways an earlier version of Katie Price – and Camilla Dallerup, a mainstay of *Strictly Come Dancing*, the programme that would have such an impact on Caroline's career (small world again). The Danish-born dancer had won *Strictly* for the first time the previous year, partnering *Holby City* actor Tom Chambers.

And, of course, there had to be new innovations to keeps the viewers tuned in, as there were every year. 'This year the infamous "bushtucker trials" are set to be the most terrifying yet and there will be plenty of new surprises to keep the celebrities on their toes every step of the way,' said a spokesman for the show, ramping up the excitement as proceedings got underway.

The arrival of the contestants was, as always, a notable event, designed to be as eye-catching as possible: this year they included sky-diving and hiking in to the base camp that was to be at the heart of the show. But more surprises were in store: when the celebrities had been in situ for five days, they were split into two teams. Each was called upon to draw a stick; the two who drew the stick with a coloured tip were named as captains. They were then called upon to choose their team members. Colin picked his partner Justin (unsurprisingly) along with Katie, Sabrina, Jimmy and Joe. Lucy picked Gino, Stuart, George, Sam and Kim. The gloves were off.

A trial then took place. Each one of the contestants was then positioned under a bucket and, using a stick, had to keep the contents of the bucket balanced by pressing down a button. The winners were the ones that had one member still standing after all the others had been knocked out; Sabrina was the lucky girl, which meant that Colin's team was the winner. As a reward they were not included in the first elimination vote and were allowed to go back to the slightly more comfortable base camp.

Base camp itself was transformed into a jungle paradise for the hungry and exhausted celebrities to relax. There were camp chairs in abundance, pillows for the beds, dressing gowns, firewood and purified water. Conditions in the jungle were regularly kept uncomfortable, both to entertain the viewers and to keep the contestants in a state of psychological anxiety, but equally, allowing some luxury while denying it to others also caused tension (great for viewing figures) between the contestants.

As a punishment for failing the task, Lucy's team entered exile camp, a rat-infested clearing containing only the bare essentials, with one log to sit on, one bed, no shower and only rice and beans to eat. No pillows, camp chairs nor indeed dressing-gowns were in evidence. Life was not a picnic for those in exile. Over the following three days, the inhabitants were called upon to take part in a 'bush battle' with the winner of each round allowed to return to base camp and gain immunity from the first public elimination vote. It was one way of causing tension between those who were taking part and, potentially, garnering some cracking televisual moments. Stuart, Kim and George were the lucky winners who were spared elimination – for now.

While the camp was split between the two parts, everyone selected for the 'bushtucker trials' competed as usual. However, there were some differences in other respects. The inhabitants of base camp were awarded the first meals, with the remainder sent on to the exiled team, another clever psychological ploy bound to raise tensions. The exception to this was a trial called 'vile vending', in which Kim competed for five 'stars' for the exiled team, while Katie competed for seven for those back at base.

This had the effect of placing increased pressure on any exiled member who completed a one-person trial, as they would have had to collect a total of twelve stars to feed their own camp. Katie, however, who was a good sport in situations like this, competed in both of them but, despite her best efforts, failed to get all stars in any of her six trials (she was to become increasingly fed up with the fact that the sadistic public kept voting for her to do the trials). On day eight the two camps reunited, and everyone was allowed to go back to base camp.

Of course, all through this, the usual eliminations took place and this year some of the celebrities chose to eliminate themselves, including Camilla, who had become ill, Katie, who was thoroughly annoyed at doing so many 'bushtucker trials' and George, who dropped out due to unspecified personal reasons. There was some bafflement about this last departure, which took place less than a week before the finale. George later confessed that the reason he had quit was that he didn't want anyone to lose out to him. He had been a big hit with the public and as a bona-fide, A-list star he felt he could well have been the winner that year. 'The last thing I wanted was to go one-on-one with people … I have too much respect for them… I just thought, Why don't I leave while I'm on a high?' he told Ant and Dec. 'As much as I would like to win, because I'm competitive, I just didn't want to see any of them lose. Sometimes you lose to win.'

At any rate, George's had been an extremely popular stint on the show, but he had been excluded from many of the trial on health grounds and was clearly missing his girlfriend, with whom he had been allowed a telephone call. He had earlier also hinted to Kim that something like this might happen. 'I feel like we are down to just a few people, all of whom I like and want to see them all benefit but I may be standing in their way: who knows, I may end up in the final three. My girl has to go back and, at this stage in my life, I have to think what is important to me in life,' he told her. 'With Christmas coming up, it makes sense to spend a few days here with my girl and go back and spend time with my kid. Time means more than anything to me now, more than money, more than life, I feel like I've lived a life and feel easy in my skin. If this was something huge for me to do or to prove something, I'd have stuck at it but I don't want to take it away from you guys.' (Or as he could have put it, but was too polite to do so, being a Hollywood A-list star was, on balance, a bigger deal than being in the jungle).

Gino was the eventual winner in a year that also saw controversy about events he was involved in on the show. He and Stuart got into trouble when they were charged by New South Wales Police after Australia's Royal Society for the Prevention of Cruelty to Animals (RSPCA) complained about their killing and eating a rat during the making of the programme. It emerged that the killing of animals for performance was illegal. ITV apologised for not having properly advised the competitors about Australian legislation regarding animal cruelty and the charges were dropped when ITV accepted responsibility for the episode. They were subsequently charged around £1,600.

Caroline excitedly reported on all this alongside fellow celebrity commentators, including former contestant Janet Street-Porter: it seemed that some of the show's old friends, at least, could hardly bear to stay away. However, there was a darker side to all that was taking place on screen: Katie, who had been popular the first time around, was no longer a hit with the viewers prior to her decision to leave the show. She received a good deal of hate mail and Caroline – who, sadly, was going to be subjected to the same kind of abuse a few years down the line – confessed, 'The emails we received about Katie were horrendous.' It should be underlined that this was happening in 2009: everyone involved in that kind of entertainment had known for a very long time that participants were often subjected to abuse and yet then, as now, there were no real controls in place.

Caroline's own stint on the show was judged to be a great success, and she was swiftly signed up for a second series. Rumours began to swirl about the enhanced television roles she might get, including hosting *The X Factor*; now twenty-eight, she was nominated for best presenter at the National Television Awards, with fellow nominees including Ant and Dec, Bruce Forsyth, Graham Norton and Cat Deeley. That was quite some company to be keeping. And she was also one of the people who actually dished out the prizes at the BT Digital Music Awards in London.

The work continued to flood in: the latest was BBC Three's *Dancing On Wheels* which was, as the title might suggest, an offshoot of *Strictly Come Dancing*. The big show was still a few years away for Caroline, but this was an early chance for her to show off her dancing prowess. The concept could not have been simpler: the idea was than an able-bodied celebrity would dance with someone in a wheelchair and each week one couple would be eliminated in a dance-off. In the final, two couples would dance twice and the winner would represent the UK in the European wheelchair dance championships. There were obvious links to *Strictly*: two of the three judges, James and Ola Jordan, were both *Strictly* regulars, as were choreographers, Brian Fortuna and Kristina Rihanoff. The third judge, Ade Adepitan, was a wheelchair basketball player and actor. The contestants were made up of six couples: Caroline danced with James O'Shea, Olympic swimmer Mark Foster was with Diana Morgan-Hill, singer Michelle Gayle was with Harry Maule, fellow singer Heather Small was with engineer and wheelchair athlete Paul Jacob, rugby league player Martin Offiah was paired with presenter Carolyne Underwood and *Hollyoaks* actor Kevin Sacre was with Simone Milani.

Somewhat inevitably, the show was dubbed in some quarters a 'wheel-ality show', but it had a serious intent and Brian Fortuna was a qualified teacher of wheelchair ballroom dancing. His mother Sandra, also a dance teacher, had developed a programme in her base in New Jersey after a couple had asked her for help with their first wedding dance. A motorcycle crash had left the groom in a wheelchair. Sandra herself flew over to see the finale and the influence on the participants was considerable. 'The lightness I feel without my legs is just incredible,' said Diana, who had lost her legs in a train accident two decades previously. 'It makes me feel how I used to when I was dancing before the accident. It takes me back to the joy of dance.' In other words, the show was having a brilliantly positive effect on people whose lives were not easy; it was a genuine boost. In the event (foreshadowing *Strictly*) Caroline and James won, with Mark and Diana the other couple in the finale .

'You've reached an excellent level of dancing in a short space of time and we think both couples would do a great job of representing us at the European Championships,' said James Jordan before the result was revealed.

'If I could, I would send both of you to the European Championships, added Ola.

Brian Fortuna said, 'I'm very proud of James and Caroline. They have achieved a great accomplishment. But they have got to work amazingly hard now to keep on a par with the rest of the European Championships.'

Caroline was elated. 'I cannot believe that me and James have won!' she said. 'We now have a great responsibility to represent the UK. No more mucking around. We're serious dancers now.' In the event they finished sixteenth in their category, a creditable performance all round.

And with that it was back off to the jungle, with the tenth series of *I'm A Celebrity* kicking off on 14 November 2010. Ant and Dec were doing the honours, as usual, with Caroline and Joe on the spin-off, along with Russell Kane, who was very much in agreement with Caroline's thinking when he declared that no way would he do a bushtucker trial.

Celebrity was as popular as ever: a few days previously, ITV officially confirmed the ten celebrities taking part: Stacey Solomon, who had risen to fame courtesy of *The X Factor*, former Happy Mondays singer Shaun Ryder, playboy model Kayla Collins, rapper Aggro Santos, Olympic sprinter Linford Christie, the nutritionist, author and television presenter Gillian McKeith, legendary actress Britt Ekland, recently unseated Liberal Democrat MP Lembit Öpik, TV personality Sheryl Gascoigne – ex-wife of footballer Paul – and smoothie-chops actor Nigel Havers. Comedian Dom Joly, comedian and novelist Jenny Eclair and presenter and former *Big Brother* star Alison Hammond did not arrive with everyone else, but were to make their entrance a few days later.

As ever, the contestants were separated, into Camp Bruce (males) and Camp Sheila (females). And there were the usual attention-catching entrance antics, this time around by skydiving or paddling in on canoes across a lake. Those who came via water then had to crawl through a damp and dark tunnel – presumably so that it wouldn't be seen as the easier option. Not that there was going to be anything easy in the jungle over the next few weeks

And so they were off and the torment (for some) began even before they entered the jungle. Contestants immediately had to undertake a five-part trial that allowed the winners one last night of luxury and sentenced the losers to a premature entrance into the jungle. The first four tasks earned the winning team one point each, the fifth and final task decided which group had to make their way into the bush.

Every series has moments that stuck with viewers and this one was no different. Highlights included Gillian McKeith becoming the second contestant in the history of the show to refuse a task (after Kerry Katona, who refused a trial in series three). She had been told that green ants and cockroaches would be dropped on her head as she operated a digger using a magnet to pick up stars for food: 'It's just too much, having things all over my head and body and trying to move the thing all at the same time,' she told Ant and Dec. 'I feel exhausted, just mental exhaustion.' Who could blame her? The wonder of it was that anyone ever agreed to do any of those trials in the first place. Her decision was greeted by a round of applause when she returned to camp but Shaun Ryder, speaking later via the bush telegraph, seemed rather less sympathetic.

'Gillian basically gave up on the trial,' he said. 'Apparently she had to use a digger. No stars means fail.'

A contrite Gillian appeared to try to make up for it later by cooking the team's beans and rice – seasoning them with some salt she had smuggled into the camp. (She tried to smuggle a lot more besides, as Caroline was to reveal.)

Dom Joly and Jenny Eclair arrived on day four and Alison Hammond appeared two days after them, the thirteenth contestant to enter the jungle, the revelation about her inclusion being made on Caroline's *I'm a Celebrity … Get Me Out of Here! NOW!* She turned up in the jungle in a crate, with the others unaware of who – or what – was inside.

For the first three days of the show, Camps Bruce and Sheila were kept apart. The camps were supposed to be equal although there were some differences in the way they were broken down between the sexes: Sheila contained a pink and white recliner, a picture of a shirtless man holding a baby and the beds were all pink. Camp Bruce, on the other hand, contained a black leather recliner, a picture of a woman scratching her bottom in tennis clothes and blue beds. Camp Bruce also was slightly bigger. (No one complained about stereotyping.) On 18 November, the two camps merged, with everyone moving into the slightly larger Camp Bruce.

The final result was that Stacey Solomon came out as the winner; Shaun Ryder was the runner-up. Only one person withdrew, Nigel Havers. Stacey's stint in the jungle resulted in something else, as well: she was to hook up with Joe Swash a few years later, with whom she remains to this day. She was also to go on to present *I'm A Celebrity … NOW!*

Gillian certainly made an impact with the viewers. She hadn't won but the most talked-about contestants often don't and she had actually been very popular. Caroline was an admirer as well. 'I love that Gillian smuggled things in her knickers,' she told the *Sunday Mirror* afterwards. 'I held all that contraband afterwards and it wouldn't fit in my handbag, let alone my knickers! There was one really long tube of salt and I asked her where she put it. Gillian replied, "Use your imagination, lass." I had a two-hour bath afterwards ... Gillian was just brilliant. I think she was better than Katie Price as Katie went in to prove a point. I really don't think Gillian knew what she was getting into.'

It was not uncommon by now for *I'm A Celebrity ... NOW!* to be making an appearance on pick-of-the-day slots in newspaper and magazine listings as much as the main programme. And as such, Caroline too was increasingly in the spotlight. She was one of five television presenters to be featured in the Irish *Mail on Sunday* talking about what it took to get to that level on television and her answers were revealing. 'When I was younger, I either wanted to be a nurse or a television presenter,' she said. 'Two complete extremes! But for me, there's nothing quite like the buzz of presenting reality TV, and working on *I'm A Celebrity* is just brilliant. I was so pleased when they invited me back this year. The whole team was fantastic – there were eight hundred of us. Ant and Dec are just lovely. Ant and I had birthdays while we were out in Australia so we had a joint celebration. With the erratic hours on the show, there isn't much opportunity for socialising, so it gave us something to look forward to ... There is definitely pressure to stay in shape. I'm very paranoid about my weight because everyone on TV is so tiny. I trained really hard and dieted for the jungle – I had to, as I'm not one of life's naturally slim people. I also can't eat before I go on air or I feel really bloated on camera – it's hard work being a girl!'

That was to be the end of Caroline's stint on *I'm A Celebrity ... NOW!*, but the exposure had the required effect in raising her even further in the public's gaze. Not that she would have enjoyed being a contestant herself: 'I worked on the 'Jungle' for two years hosting the ITV2 spin-off show and I can safely say you would not get me in there,' she told Mailonline some years later, adding, 'I'm not very good with creepy-crawlies, water or heights.' She didn't need to be. She was in demand for such a lot of work now, not just television presenting but often modelling – ironically enough, for someone who had been as insecure about her body as she had as a child. Routinely referred to as 'leggy', she also regularly made 'world's sexiest' lists and new pictures of her wearing clothes that showed off her figure would always provoke quite a response from the fans. For Caroline, it was upwards and onwards. The world was at her designer-shod feet.

6

A REAL X FACTOR

There was a very good reason Caroline was not going back to the jungle: she was too much in demand.

For a start, between her jungle stints, she had spent a few months on *The Whole 19 Yards*, a short-lived game show hosted by Vernon Kay. Caroline was the 'games guru', watching over four contestants who had to compete in three rounds involving general knowledge questions and physical challenges. They used buzzers that started to move to the opposite end of the stage and the contestants had to rush further across to reach them, traversing a challenge course as they went to stop them moving any further. Correct answers increased the contestants' winnings from £5,000 up to a total of £100,000 and, if the buzzer moved the total nineteen yards, the contestant lost everything. On paper, it could be seen why the game could have generated some excitement, but it didn't really catch the viewers' imagination. Neither did the international versions tried out in Austria, Brazil, Germany and Spain.

But Caroline was as busy as ever. She took part in a modelling shoot for *Maxim*, which described her as 'bubblier than a fresh pint of Foster's top', while Caroline herself admitted, 'I was extremely nervous. I don't usually get pictured in my knickers in front of ten or more people. It's not something I usually do. But I eased into it and by the end of the day I was running around being silly.' It was proof positive that all that insecurity about her looks and much else wasn't shared by anyone else – but still Caroline continued to harbor angst. Not that you would have been able to tell. On the surface and in public she was as lively and fun as she had ever been.

She was a good sport, too. In the interview she talked about being rock'n'roll – 'Do you know what? I'm generally quite a good girl. I used to have a habit of dancing on bars when I got drunk, which was fun. And I once got caught having a shower by Taylor Hawkins, from the Foo Fighters. Is that rock'n'roll? Being caught having a shower? … I was backstage at V Festival. It was an accident.'

And her first gig? 'Lenny Kravitz at Wembley when I was fifteen. He was brilliant. I was right at the back but I could see everything … I even lied to my friends that I touched his hair. It's a big thing going to Wembley when you come from a little village in Norfolk, so I just made up these stories.'

And the most famous rock star she'd ever met? Caroline herself had been moving in these circles for a long time now, but still she managed to come across as ditzy as any fan. 'Dave Grohl. I was so nervous,' she said. 'He was in his changing room and I had to go and say, "Hello," but I didn't think what I was going to say next, so I just went in and said, "Hello," and had nothing else to say. We just stood there awkwardly looking at each other. He must have thought, Who's this random idiot? And then I just said, "Bye," and walked off. Brilliant – well done me.' That was Caroline through and through – self-deprecating, able to laugh at herself and not taking the whole rock chick number too seriously.

She was being taken seriously by others, though – she presented backstage at the 2010 Brit Awards for ITV2, another sign that she was an established presence in showbiz circles. That show, incidentally, played host to Liam Gallagher, who thanked all his bandmates with the exception of his brother Noel before throwing his microphone into the audience, thus causing a ten-minute delay while everyone searched for it. The host of the evening, Peter Kay, was not amused.

There was another short-lived game show: *Minute To Win It*, which originated in the USA and spawned various versions in over fifty different countries worldwide. The UK version was different from that in the States. There were teams captained by Caroline and her old friend Joe Swash – the Stripes and the Spots respectively – with five contestants each, girls on Caroline's team and boys on Joe's. The names were a nod to Cadbury, which sponsored the show while also promoting its involvement in the London 2012 Olympics with an ad campaign called 'Spots v Stripes'.

The teams competed in six games – either head-to-head or solo against the clock – to win points. Each contestant could only play once, except for the team captains, who appeared twice, once for a solo game and once for a two-player game. After those initial battles, the highest scoring team got to play games that led to the cash prize round. The first game built up a fund with every point scored, and the second determined whether or not that team won the money. The maximum on offer was £30,000.

Caroline, as always, proved herself to be a very good sport as a captain. Elsewhere, she was a sought-after guest, too, appearing on *Loose Women*, as a panelist on *Sweat The Small Stuff*, as a contestant on *Who Wants to be a Millionaire Celebrity Family Special* and in a cameo role on *Lemon La Vida Loca*. This last was a mock reality show created by Caroline's old mate Leigh Francis, aka television personality Keith Lemon, which purported to follow his home and work life. Quite a few well known personalities were persuaded to play themselves: alongside Caroline, there were numerous others, including Kelly Brook, Jodie Marsh, Danny Dyer, Stacey Solomon, Holly Willoughby, Gary Barlow and many more. This was the regular set in which Caroline found herself.

And the bigger gigs kept on coming, propelling her further into the limelight, with one of the biggest shows of all now in her sights – to say nothing of the very unexpected consequences it would have for her personal life. *The X Factor* had been created by Simon Cowell way back in 2004 with the idea of finding new singing talent. Over the years the great and the good of British show business had turned up on the judging panel; apart from Simon himself, they included Sharon Osbourne, Louis Walsh, Dannii Minogue, Cheryl Tweedy, Gary Barlow, Mel B., Louis Tomlinson and Robbie Williams. And the show had created some genuine stars, among them Leona Lewis, Matt Cardle, Alexandra Burke, Little Mix, One Direction and Olly Murs. Those last two were to be of particular interest to Caroline.

The accompanying show, *The Xtra Factor*, also dated back to 2004 (in 2015 it was renamed *The Xtra Factor Live* before finishing in 2016) and was created to replicate the success of *Big Brother's Little Brother*. Broadcast on ITV2 on Saturday and Sunday nights after the main show, it featured behind-the-scenes footage from the main show itself, as well as focusing on the contestants' responses when the judges commented on their performances. It also contained extra auditions, competitions and games, a celebrity panel that would provide comment on the proceedings, and live video calls and phone calls with the judges and contestants. And it featured the usual merry-go-round from Planet Celebrity, of which Caroline was now firmly a part.

Originally, the show was presented by Ben Shephard, until Fearne Cotton took over for series four. She was followed by the ubiquitous Holly Willoughby and the ex-*Blue Peter* presenter Konnie Huq. It was felt, perhaps, that the show was going a little flat and there were rumours that Konnie would be dropped until she took matters into her own hands and announced she would be leaving due to a clash of filming schedules. Her new vehicle, a show for the Discovery Channel in China, was now going to be taking up much of her time.

Quite a few names were in the frame to take over. These included Girls Aloud star Kimberley Walsh and Sky Sports presenter Georgie Thompson. BBC Radio 1 host Matt Edmondson was also said to be in the running and, when he wasn't on the final list, he took it in good form. 'Got my bag packed, train tickets booked to Birmingham, copy of Simon's autobiography!' he tweeted.' Can't wait!... What's that you say? OLLY MURS?!??!?! Thank God I'm still in the running for *Countdown*.'

For, yes, it was indeed Olly, a 2009 contestant on the show and now a successful singer, with hits such as 'Please Don't Let Me Go', who would be presenting, alongside one Caroline Flack. The news was announced via Twitter, as was usual these days, and it had generated a good deal of enthusiasm behind the scenes. An *Xtra Factor* insider told the *Mirror*, 'We're really excited about Caroline and Olly fronting the show. Unfortunately, things fell a bit flat last year but it is going to be back with a bang. Caroline is a very talented presenter and she'll be perfect for the show, while Olly is already hugely popular with *The X Factor* audience.' It was to be a match made in televisual heaven – although not one, much to the viewers' chagrin, that would ever spill into real life.

Just a few days previously, the judging panel for the main show had been announced: Louis Walsh, Take That's Gary Barlow, Destiny's Child singer Kelly Rowland and N-Dubz singer Tulisa Contostavlos. Over on *Xtra*, Olly was also talking it up: 'I'm so excited to be joining the *Xtra Factor* with Caroline,' he said. '*The X Factor* is the show that put me where I am, so I'm chuffed to be involved again – this time to work on it from the other side and see some new stars coming through.'

And Caroline, who was now an old pro in presenting spin-offs, added, 'I'm a massive fan of *The X Factor* and can't wait to get started. I'm sad to leave the jungle but I've had a great two years and this is an opportunity that I couldn't turn down.'

The X Factor, of course, was named after that special-something quality that set a star performer apart from the rest. But in Caroline's case it could also have referred to the various romantic frissons that seemed to accompany her, because there was more than one. First up was Olly himself. The pair sparked off each other on screen, so much so that people thought they really were a couple. A few years later the pair gave a joint interview to *Heat* magazine about those early days that revealed how they had managed to set the screen alight:

Caroline: 'That was a little bit flirty.'

Olly: 'We were both single at the time.'

Caroline: 'I did fancy you when we first started.'

Olly: 'I used to watch you on *I'm A Celebrity ... Get Me Out of Here NOW!*, and thought you seemed like a top person. Someone really lovely, who I could go out for a drink and have a laugh with. It's almost like when you think of girlfriends – you're the perfect girlfriend.'

Caroline: [Deadpan] 'Basically, I'm your perfect girl.'

Olly: 'I think all guys look at you in that way.'

A fair few certainly thought that Olly did. The chemistry between the couple was clearly one of the reasons their stint together worked so well. And right from the start fans were (wrongly) convinced there was an off-screen romance and named the two Colly Flurs. Some years later Olly broke up with his long-term girlfriend and many were convinced that Caroline was the reason: 'All I get is, "You're the reason that Olly and his girlfriend broke up, la-la-la!"' she told *Red* magazine. 'But I haven't done anything! We have this weird chemistry and an innate understanding. It's not sexual but it's not platonic either. I do love him. It's kind of like we're married but we don't have sex – like most marriages, then!'

With that kind of response, was it any wonder that people were curious? Olly was just as bad. He gave a very provocative interview to the *Sun* while the show was on the air which made it clear quite how well they got on: 'I get to work with *The X Factor*, which is the best show on TV, and I get to work with someone gorgeous like Caroline,' he said. 'Happy days. We get to have a laugh and a cuddle all day and we have a kiss here and there. We get on well and it's great to have chemistry both on camera and off.' But nothing had happened! But, then again, it might ... 'Sometimes relationships build over time and at the moment we're concentrating on the job in hand, but we do have a good flirt,' he said. 'She's attractive and we have a laugh so when the show finishes in December who knows what will happen?'

Given all that, was it any wonder the viewers had them down as pairing off behind the scenes? And it all made for sensational publicity for the show, of course. The would-they/wouldn't-they element has been used since time immemorial to get viewers to tune into a show and it usually works, as long as the uncertainty can be maintained. Conventional wisdom has it that that was the reason Ross and Rachel kept breaking up in *Friends*: take the tension out of the equation and the hold on the viewer is no longer the same.

That wasn't to say that the presenters were not for real: both Caroline and Olly clearly thought there was a chance it might work out. 'There was a point when we first started working together when I thought, Do I? Could I? There's always been a barrier where we just couldn't ever cross that line and we never have,' Caroline told the *Daily Telegraph*. 'I've never met anyone as confident in my whole life but it never borders on arrogance. It's quite extraordinary. His confidence is lovely – I wish I had that, [being] confident about everything I do. He never moans, he's got energy, he's constantly up.' It was telling, though, that remark about having confidence – the insecurity was still there. Caroline was getting very, very good at covering it but there were hints that not all was well in her life.

But for now, Caroline was on the verge of her next relationship, one that would have the nation's eyebrows shooting through the roof at the sheer unlikeliness, and would knock the speculation about Olly into a cocked hat. One of the contestants on *The X Factor* the previous year had been a boy band that had gone on to become internationally famous, with a major hit, 'What Makes You Beautiful', and had a huge future. The band was One Direction and its lead singer was one Harry Styles. Very good-looking, in a boyish way, with a shock of brown hair, sometimes worn long, and an increasing predilection for tattoos, Harry was destined to be a major heart-throb. In fact, he would be compared to Mick Jagger. But back then the main focus was on how boyish he was.

Born 1 February 1994 (when Caroline was already in her teens), brought up in Cheshire and with divorced parents, Harry had initially auditioned for *The X Factor* in 2010 as a solo singer. On that occasion he had been eliminated, but he was brought back to form the boy band One Direction with four bandmates, all of whom had also originally auditioned as solo singers. None of them made the grade alone (back then, at least – they were later to create successful solo careers) but together they were stronger than the sum of their parts.

Five was a perfect number for a boy band and the genre had been an extremely lucrative proposition over the years – just ask Take That, the Jonas Brothers or Westlife. Get it right on a talent programme and everyone benefitted. In this case, that was the band, the show that discovered them and Simon Cowell himself, who would be signing them to his label, Syco. And the boys worked well together: there were even suggestions that it was Caroline herself who had suggested putting Harry in the group, although the reality has been lost in the mists of time. Simon Cowell and guest judge Nicole Scherzinger both also laid claim to the idea. But whoever suggested it – it worked.

In the year since they won, the boys had become very big stars. And they were making good use of their new-found fame. Harry, who had achieved major desirability status, had developed a crush on Caroline and was making no secret of it: 'Frankie [Bridge of The Saturdays] and Caroline Flack are my favourites. They are both hot,' he told *Daily Star Sunday*. He followed that up with a comment on *The X Factor*'s website: 'If Caroline Flack is reading this, say "Hi" from me. She is gorgeous!' It was said that he was roping *The Xtra Factor* producer Tim Dean in, asking him to send a tweet to Caroline asking for a date.

In the event, Harry was able to ask for a date himself. *The X Factor* held an after-show party at W Hotel in October and the lovebirds were both present. Caroline had spoken of how she already knew Harry fancied her – he had hardly been keeping it a secret – and with that the relationship began. It was Harry who had pursued Caroline, and not the other way around, but that was not going to protect her from very unfair accusations about predatory behaviour. Both were keen to keep their relationship from Simon Cowell (initially, at least) on the grounds that both were working for him and it might have made things tricky. But given his own ability to generate headlines, Cowell might well have been absolutely delighted at the news. All publicity is good publicity, after all.

It could hardly have been a more unlikely pairing. Caroline was thirty-two and Harry was seventeen. It was, indeed, due to that age gap that some people took a little while to believe the relationship was happening at all: it was only when both were pictured leaving each other's flats in the morning that the rumour mill began to generate stories in earnest. Harry was said to be devastated when Caroline flew off without him to spend a month in India. 'She's his first big relationship,' confided a friend. At that age, was it any surprise? Like it or not, eyebrows really were raised, not least because no one could remember a famous woman in her thirties dating a famous man not yet out of his teens before. There was nothing illegal going on and both worked in the world of show business, but there were murmurs of concern. No matter: the two of them got on with it, and Caroline's twin Jody was tasked with driving Harry to King's Cross station to catch a train and meet his band in Sheffield (her children were in the back of the car and must have been thrilled). He was said to have met Caroline's folks.

'Harry has met the family and they fully approve,' a source told the *Sunday People*. 'They think Harry is a lovely bloke and see that he makes Caroline very happy. She clearly misses him when he goes away but it's only for a few nights. It was very telling of how serious the relationship is that Jody has taken to driving them around. Things are really going well for Harry and Caroline. He can't believe that he has pulled her. It's pretty serious between them now.'

Caroline was not immune from being teased by her fellow celebrities about the age gap. She occasionally appeared on *Never Mind The Buzzcocks*, once shortly after the relationship had come to light. Guest host Rhod Gilbert referenced the fact they had been spotted kissing: 'She's a thirty-something TV presenter rumoured to be dating Harry Styles after they shared a love of food,' he said. 'She taught him to eat an oyster – he gave her a mouthful of his McFlurry.' Caroline looked embarrassed but it didn't end there: her team was asked to sing one line from 'What Makes You Beautiful', a song Caroline plainly didn't know. But she was a good sport about it, tweeting the programme afterwards. Twitter was already playing a big role in her life and it was going to go on to do more.

The debate over the lopsided ages raged. Many defended her. Harry was not a child and, given the impact One

Direction had had on the world, he was already living an extraordinary life with experiences most men twice his age wouldn't have had. Most pop stars had private lives that at some stages at least are 'colourful'; moreover, it was said to be the aim of many a young boy to find a mature older women to initiate them into the arts of love. In France, they made a national pastime of it. Was what the two of them were doing really so wrong?

But then there was Caroline's stated wish of having a stable relationship. Could this be it? Caroline was making no secret of her desire to follow in her sister's footsteps and find a life partner with whom to have children. 'One day I'd love to settle down with someone,' she told *Fabulous* magazine. I'd like my twin sister Jo's life. She's got a lovely partner, a gorgeous house and two kids. That's definitely the next step for me.'

But could it be Harry? In truth, the answer was 'No'. A fourteen-year age gap might not have mattered that much if both were older to begin with, but Harry was still a teenager – and one experiencing international stardom at that – and there was no way he was going to want to settle down at that stage. Nor was there any indication whatsoever that Caroline really thought this one would work out in the longer term. She laughed off the age difference at the time, saying that she felt like she was still eighteen (and certainly she looked far younger than her real age) and pointed out that they were having fun with this partnering, but for the first time ever, begun to attract genuinely negative comment, both in the mainstream press and in the cesspits of social media. Caroline was defiant, but this was not the reaction she was used to and, somewhat ominously, the episode led to her increasing obsession with Twitter, constantly monitoring what people were saying. It also meant she had to move house because her front door led straight out into the street and an ever-present group of waiting photographers.

It got to be too much. Somewhat inevitably the couple parted around the new year of 2012 – both acknowledged that it had really just been a bit of fun and, later that year, Harry had a brief fling with Taylor Swift (a mere stripling at twenty-two), although he would go on to be associated with other older women. Caroline herself briefly left Twitter, but – unfortunately for her – returned. She remained very defiant, though, about the relationship, telling the *Sun*, 'I will live my life the way I want to. And I will never judge others for living the life they want to live. The last thing I'm going to do is live my life according to anybody else. And I'm not coming off Twitter. I have fun on Twitter. I use it for having a bit of a laugh and have got the loveliest followers. A lot of them are One Direction fans. So it's not all One Direction fans who've, y'know … it's a minority.' It had been getting very dark, though: a One Direction fan magazine showed her as a voodoo doll, while another tweeter threatened to shoot her. It would have taken the hide of a rhino – which Caroline did not have – not to mind.

Even so she was capable of seeing just how bizarre the whole thing was. 'The best one I got said, "F**k you, I can't believe you're going out with my boyfriend, I hope you get eaten by an angry elephant." An angry elephant? You've just got to think these people are in front of their computers and probably don't think you even see it half the time. I just don't think anyone deserves to be bullied. That's just not on.'

Who would disagree? But it happened in person, too: strangers on the street had been shouting 'Paedophile!' at her, despite the fact that Harry was not a child, and 'pervert'. It couldn't have done anything but hurt anyone in that position. There were also a lot of rumours about how their relationship had ended, prompting Harry himself to take to Twitter: 'Please know I didn't "dump" Caroline,' he said. 'This was a mutual decision. She is one of the kindest, sweetest people I know. Please respect that.' His mother, by all accounts, liked her. His father Des was said to be relieved the pair were no more.

It was the scrutiny that was hardest to bear. Caroline was used to being in the spotlight by now, but not with the intensity she had experienced this time. She had 'learned a difficult lesson' she told the *People*, although the lesson itself involved not being too public about her romances. The sheer force of it all seemed to astonish her. So did the sheer nastiness with which she was faced.

After the split, Caroline was offered half a million pounds to be the face of a cougar website – 'cougars' being the term for women who date much younger men – which can't have cheered her up either, and in her autobiography she reflected that perhaps she and Harry had done the wrong thing. But nothing justified the abuse. And no one had really done anything wrong: 'We got very close for a time – but that's between me and Harry,' she told the *Daily Star Sunday* in the aftermath of the relationship. 'Then we decided it was best to be just friends. Harry is adorable. He is a nice person. He was nice to me, we were nice to each other. We are still friends, he's brilliant and he's so much fun.'

But it seemed she was developing a more philosophical bent, a few years later writing a letter in *Cosmopolitan* magazine to her past life. 'Dear men of my thirties,' she wrote. 'I dated friends and I dated younger men and I dated men who were hopelessly inappropriate and it was all … fun.

Dating as a thirty-something woman felt more powerful than dating in my twenties – and all you guys made me see that. By your thirties, you've survived heartbreak, you've survived long, messy relationships, you've survived unrequited love and maddening love that leaves you tired and confused and willing to give it all up.' This was seen as a direct reference to Harry, although the two were to remain friends, even if the relationship didn't survive.

If her love life was raising eyebrows, her professional life certainly wasn't. It was confirmed that she would be returning to the next series of *The Xtra Factor* in 2012 – 'London excelled in loveliness today!' she tweeted. 'Super delighted that I'm back working on *Xtra Factor* with Olly … will miss him in auditions' – which, quite apart from anything else, was a sign that her employers certainly didn't object to her relationship choices and were providing their full support.

And so the ninth series of *The X Factor* kicked off, with a comforting return to the format that worked so well: Louis Walsh, Gary Barlow, Tulisa and Nicole Scherzinger were judges along with various guests; Barlow mentored the over-twenty-eights, Walsh the groups, Tulisa the girls and Nicole the boys. A trailer for the new series, 'Whose Time Is It Now?', featured past contestants talking about how the show changed their lives; it included One Direction. Ratings were not as good as previously, but a new crop of stars were nevertheless unleashed to roam free. The eventual winner was James Arthur, who had the show's biggest ever single, a cover of Shontelle's 'Impossible', also enjoyed Caroline cooing over his performances. She told *Metro*, 'When he sings, it gets you there and I don't think we've had that before with an *X Factor* contestant. It's almost like you want to fix him a little bit.' But he was not the only star to emerge.

Rylan Clark-Neal, Union J (another boy band who originally auditioned as a three-piece before adding another member) and Ella Henderson were out of the stables that year, all going on to forge successful careers as well as mingling in the show business world that was Caroline's own.

And, indeed, there was something of an X-factor between Caroline and James: the pair's names were linked, although both denied that any romance took place. But James was clearly keen, saying, 'I think Caroline Flack is beautiful. Maybe we'll see in the future. Things like this have to develop.' At least he was closer to her in age at all of twenty-four. But Caroline wasn't interested, despite her fulsome praise for his performance and despite the fact that the two were occasionally pictured out together just, as they emphasised, as friends. Her search for love was still ongoing. And there was so much on the cards these days: as a fully-fledged inhabitant of Planet Celeb, Caroline was now asked to be involved in charitable campaigns and, of course, she agreed. She was photographed with no make-up for Children In Need's 'Bearfaced' (just proving that she looked sensational with no make-up). She was constantly in demand.

And that included her presence in the tenth series of *The Xtra Factor* in 2013, although change was also on the way. Olly had decided he'd had enough: it was a 'lot of pressure,' he said. 'It's going to be a shame not to do *The Xtra Factor* again. I'm gutted because it's been a huge part of my life for the last two years. But I think whoever Caroline decides to pick, whoever the bosses decide to pick to replace me, is going to be great. I don't know if she would do it on her own. We'll see what happens in the future. I mean, you never know. I don't get four weeks' holiday a year – I only get one week or two weeks sometimes – and I don't get weekends off like everyone else. I have missed that. Fundamentally, you need time off to refresh your memory and brain. I love it, but it is a lot of pressure.'

Olly was replaced by Matt Richardson, a comedian and broadcaster, but it just wasn't the same. There had been speculation that without Olly, Caroline herself might not want to return, but while she seemed as bubbly and enthusiastic as ever, she did not return for the following series and was ultimately replaced by Sarah-Jane Crawford. 'I have a little announcement,' she said cheerily. 'After three brilliant years of hosting *Xtra Factor*, it's time to pass the baton. It's been incredible and I'll never forget it. How can I when I am married to Louis Walsh? It's all he ever talks about at home. I wish the new team all the best and look forward to watching the new series.'

She was joking, of course. The search for love went on.

7

DANCING TO GLORY

Caroline was now in demand across the board and that included the charity sector. Her high profile meant that she was able to shine a light on good works and important projects that might otherwise have stayed under the radar.

Those who knew Caroline spoke often of her extremely generous spirit and goodness of heart: it was hardly surprising, then, that she became involved in a number of good causes. She had previously done some work for Children In Need and in 2014 she got on board with Sport Relief, the year it raised £71.8 million (including government aid) to help some of the poorest people in the world.

An offshoot of Comic Relief since 2002 (somewhat appropriately, given Caroline's frequent association with television offshoots), Sport Relief alternated with its older sibling every other year in March. The annual live telethon was broadcast live from the Queen Elizabeth Olympic Park for the first time and was hosted by Gary Lineker, David Walliams, Davina McCall, Fearne Cotton, Jack Whitehall and Claudia Winkleman. A feature called Clash Of The Titans was hosted by Gabby Logan and Clare Balding, while the teams were headed by John Bishop and Sebastian Coe. The Sport Relief Mile was joined by three major cycling events in London, Manchester and Glasgow and more than six hundred swimathons.

Right from the start, Comic and Sport Relief had been associated with sub-Saharan Africa – that was why they had been set up – and this year was to be no different, with much aid going to Rwanda, among other countries. Caroline had only been a young teenager when the horrific genocide in that country took place in 1994, but the ramifications were still being felt two decades later, with a population that was still largely in shock over the horrors that had gone on and was building itself up again from the devastation left behind. Many children had been orphaned and as such had had no one to teach them the basic skills they needed to survive – such as how to farm. International aid organisations had become involved to help not only individuals but the entire country in its recovery.

And so Caroline headed out to visit the wonderful World Jewish Relief project, which had teamed up with local partner Uyisenga Ni Imanzi (Family For Every Child) on the ground in Rwanda. They were helping orphaned survivors of the conflict to use their land well by training them to set up farming co-operatives. The beneficiaries were taught both good farming practice and also how to run a business, with the aim of allowing them to support themselves and their families.

Everyone involved agreed that Caroline carried off her Sport Relief reporting well, managing to strike exactly the right note of sympathy and balancing that with the sense of liveliness required to engage the viewer. 'I met some amazing men and women who went through the most horrendous experiences during the genocide,' she said. 'It was incredibly emotional hearing their stories. But thanks to support from the project, their lives are now changing for the better. They are learning how to grow crops and sell their produce, providing a better livelihood not just for themselves, but also their families and even the wider community. It's all about giving people a leg-up rather than a handout. The work that the project is doing is brilliant and so inspiring – it really is transforming lives. I've always been a huge supporter of Sport Relief so it's fantastic to see how the cash raised from this year's campaign is already helping to give communities in Rwanda a better future.' The team also included Dee Koppang, Dermot O'Leary's wife and a freelance television and film producer; the two were pictured together with local children.

It was invaluable publicity for an extremely worthy project as Caroline was pictured out in the field with local farmers as they were being shown how to form their co-operatives to sell their produce. She didn't complain, spending long hours in the broiling sun and listening to the sometimes harrowing stories. 'I saw how the project, World Jewish Relief, supported by cash raised for Sport Relief, has been helping these makeshift families to start a business from their farmland, forming co-operatives that would sell fruit and vegetables to make a good profit. They've built a new life from scratch,' Caroline told *Marie Claire*. 'For many people, growing the odd vegetable is a nice hobby. Here in Rwanda, these plantations are a real lifeline; a source of income that's not only transforming the lives of the co-operative members but also their entire communities.' She lamented the fact that, back at home, she struggled to keep even a pot plant alive.

She also talked about the strength of the women she met, citing one named Judith, who lost all her family in the genocide and who went on to take care of orphans and run a farming co-operative. 'I also met a group of women survivors who spend every day working barefoot on one of the local farms, some of them with their young children strapped to their back,' she said. 'Between picking tomatoes and mulching watermelons in the baking sun, they still had the energy to burst into laughter at my feeble attempts to help.'

In the wake of Caroline's tragic death, Ekaterina Mitiaev, who works with World Jewish Relief and had been involved with the trip, remembered how much Caroline had brought to the table. Far from being a high-maintenance diva celeb, she had given it her all. 'Caroline immediately proved herself to be hardworking and professional,' Ekaterina blogged in *The Times of Israel*. 'We took her deep into the Rwandan countryside, where she had to stand for long periods under a hot sun while filming. She joined farmers in tomato fields and spent time harvesting, carrying the basket on her shoulder and helping to load the truck.'

It was all a far cry from her life back in Britain, which was continuing to do well on a professional level. Earlier in the year, Caroline had been the presenter of a show called *Viral Tap*, a comedy panel game in which viewers sent in videos that had the potential to go viral and which could earn them £250, £500 or £1,000 in prize money. It also featured panellists Matt Richardson and Carly Smallman, with Jim Chapman as another presenter. The idea was that the videos should be eye-catching and the best ones would earn the good money. 'I'm very excited and proud to be presenting *Viral Tap*,' said Caroline. 'It's going to fun working with my panel; my old pal Matt and the lovely Carly who is equally hilarious. We're looking forward to sharing some mind-boggling clips with you all and pretty much spending the whole show laughing.' It only ran for one series but her profile continued to rise.

Her personal life seemed to be on an even keel, too. Caroline had started dating Jack Street, manager of Sam Smith and the electric duo Disclosure, and it had seemed to be getting serious, with Jack moving in with her. He was eight years younger but, in this case, it was an age gap that did not raise eyebrows (although it did give rise to more 'cougar' comments and the odd joke). The two had flirted openly on Twitter, Jack had been seen watching her during some recordings on television and Caroline had tweeted pictures of him getting rid of a daddy long-legs from her flat. They attended Glastonbury together. But it was not to last and, in fact, would go on to result in some extreme and long-lasting unhappiness on Caroline's part.

Outside of work, she had become quite the accomplished DJ and, despite her self-confessed tendency to moan about festivals, thoroughly enjoyed attending them too. Now an acknowledged beauty, Caroline could have passed for much younger than her thirty-four years; physically tiny and with size two feet, she had developed something of a signature look, often sporting shorts to show off her impressive pins. The days of bulking out tights to make her legs look bigger were long gone. And it was in late summer that rumours began that Caroline was to appear on *Strictly Come Dancing*, as referenced at the beginning of this book.

It was in August 2014 that it was confirmed that Caroline was going to appear on *Strictly* on the BBC. It came at a good time: despite her good-humoured departure, Caroline had been disappointed about losing her *Xtra Factor* gig and not only was *Strictly* a very high-profile role, but it took her up against her old crowd, including Simon Cowell, over on ITV. The press was full of interest in this potential showdown, while the BBC was pleased at its coup. 'Producers think Caroline is very pretty and has bags of sex appeal,' a BBC source told the *Mirror*. 'She has a young fanbase and executives are hoping she will bring in younger viewers to help beat *The X Factor*'s viewer numbers. It's also a bit of a snub to the ITV talent show as Caroline is now going to be in a BBC programme that is a direct rival.' Caroline herself was aware of the two formats squaring up but she did not encourage the rivalry: when she called *Strictly* the best show on television, she quickly realised how this could be interpreted in *The X Factor* camp and got in touch with Simon Cowell to make amends. And indeed, her links with *The X Factor* were far from severed.

The news of her participation on the show was actually broken by accident by Caroline's replacement on *The Xtra Factor*, Sarah-Jane Crawford. 'Lovely catching up with @ carolineflack1 this AM, drinks soon twinkle toes? Now smash Strictly #girlpower,' she tweeted, before realising she'd jumped the gun and swiftly deleting the tweet.

The full list was soon released, including stars and the professional dancers they were to be matched with: Gregg Wallace was to be paired with Aliona Vilani, Jennifer Gibney with Tristan MacManus, Tim Wonnacott with Natalie Lowe, Thom Evans with Iveta Lukosiute, Scott Mills with Joanne Clifton, Alison Hammond with Aljaž Škorjanec, Judy Murray with Anton du Beke, Steve Backshall with Ola Jordan, Sunetra Sarker with Brendon Cole, Pixie Lott with Trent Whiddon, Jake Wood with Janette Manrara, Mark

Wright with Karen Hauer, Frankie Bridge with Kevin Clifton and Simon Webbe with Kristina Rihanoff. And finally, of course, Caroline with Pasha Kovalev. By now a veteran of several series of *Strictly*, Pasha had previously moved from Russia to the USA and had been in the UK since 2011. The competition commenced.

The presenters were Tess Daly and Claudia Winkleman: this was the first year there was to be no Sir Bruce Forsyth on hand, the long-running presenter of *Strictly*, although he did make one final appearance at the show's launch, as well as continuing to host the Christmas and Children In Need specials. Zoe Ball was presenting *Strictly Come Dancing: It Takes Two* on BBC Two, while the judges were Len Goodman, Bruno Tonioli, Craig Revel Horwood and Darcy Bussell, with Donny Osmond putting in a guest stint. Zoe stepped across the channels to stand in as a presenter herself, when Claudia had to step away for family reasons. With the line-up complete and still one of the BBC's most popular shows, *Strictly* was to prove a hit once more. The other celebs did their bit in cranking up interest by giving interviews about their forthcoming participation in the show.

'I'm so excited to be doing *Strictly*, it's going to be a lot of fun. I always want to push myself as a performer so can't wait to learn the routines,' said singer Pixie Lott. It would be his 'wildest challenge', said naturalist Steve Backshall. The Saturdays' vocalist Frankie Bridge was equally enthused. 'I'm such a huge fan of *Strictly*! I've always wanted to be a part of the show – it looks like so much fun and the costumes are just gorgeous. Like so many little girls, I used to take dance lessons when I was in primary school and I really love dancing, but this is going to be so different from anything I have done with The Saturdays. I just can't wait to get started!'

'I'm so happy to be doing the show,' said rugby star Thom Evans. 'I cannot wait to get started. I'm really looking forward to my *Strictly* makeover – bring on *Strictly* and bring on the spandex.' Bring on the spandex they did. There were a few complaints that the contestants were not quite as famous as the crew had been in previous years, but equally, there was soon comment about quite how glamorous the contingent was that year. And that even included the men.

Caroline opened up about being paired off with Pasha in an interview she gave to the *Radio Times* a year later, revealing the pressures and strains everyone was under from the start. To begin with, there was the issue of pairing the celebrity with their professional partner, which was not as straightforward as it might seem on screen. 'It's almost like a quick speed-dating, in terms of the dancing,' she said. 'The girls stand in a circle and the boys are in the outer circle and they dance around you and then they go swap – boom – swap – boom – and then they film it and sort of see who's good with who … We absolutely hands-down do not know. And I knew I wanted Pasha, and they gave him to me in the dress run, so I was gutted as I was, like, well, if they've given him to me in the dress run, I'm not going to get him. I was like gutted, gutted, gutted, and I was thinking, Well, I'm not going to get Pasha – who am I going to get? You just don't know. Then they obviously double-bluffed and they gave him to me and I screamed.' As with Olly, she shared an on-screen chemistry with her dancing partner with whom she worked (and danced) well. Pasha was also to prove very understanding when times started to get tough.

At the outset Pixie was the firm favourite to win: viewers did not know that Caroline had trained as a dancer and, initially at least, she played it down. It then emerged that

Pixie was also a trained dancer, having studied at the Italia Conti Academy of Theatre Arts.

'Behind this very curtain your celebrities are waiting. Pros, are you ready?' asked Tess. Caroline stood out at the launch, sporting a pair of trademark shorts. She opened the show and, despite her nerves, got a standing ovation . The more perceptive among the audience and viewers at home realised quite quickly that she and Pixie were by far the most talented of the lot. Both got twenty-seven points in their first week. At first, though, Pixie appeared to have the edge, but not for long.

Any complaints about the contestants not being famous enough were soon forgotten. Viewers were thoroughly enjoying the spectacle, not least because some mischievous behind-the-scenes person clearly could not resist reminding Caroline of her past. The producers set her pre-performance segment to the song 'Steal My Girl', which just happened to be by One Direction, prompting a Twitter deluge ('that's awk'), which Caroline rose above. (Mostly – she was sometimes to show her exasperation that people would still not stop going on about Harry Styles.) And her dancing was getting better and better. By October she was really showing her worth, scoring well and prompting Len Goodman to call a quickstep to 'We Go Together' from *Grease* the 'best dance of tonight.'

Countdown star Rachel Riley was a previous *Strictly* contestant and was now going out with Pasha (they were to go on to marry and have a child). She was very generous about her boyfriend's dancing partner. 'I think Caroline and Pasha will win,' she said loyally to the *Daily Express*. 'As soon as I saw their first dance I thought, Wow. I think she's amazing and I know how much effort they've put into training – as do all of them. She's a really good dancer so it's really nice to see the choreography done justice.'

And she was also impressed by DJ Scott Mills. 'I hope Scott's not [going]. He's not even been in the bottom two yet. The thing about *Strictly* is you never know – you have to vote for your favourite because there's a curse of the middle ground. That's what happened when I was out and quite a few of the contestants at the moment have been in the middle, and you hope that you're safe. The top are safe anyway, the bottom know they need a vote. So if you like watching someone dance then vote for them. I like watching Scott and I know he's really enjoying it so I hope he doesn't go out.' Rachel was clearly more engaged than most, given that it was her boyfriend dancing up there on the screen, but like so many *Strictly* contestants, up to and including Caroline herself, she remained fascinated by the show. It seemed to exert a strange hold over those people who took part; even years afterwards they kept a close eye on the proceedings as the new crowd danced on.

Scott Mills did not, in fact, last on the show much longer and, as the contestants began to leave, the tension mounted. Caroline was herself doing ever better. And there was more good news – she, Alison Hammond, Mark Wright, Thom Evans and Frankie Bridge were all confirmed for the *Strictly* tour the following year. 'My *Strictly* experience so far has been amazing and doing the tour lets me carry on dancing a little longer,' said Caroline. It was announced that the tour would kick off at the Barclaycard Arena, Birmingham, on 16 January the following year, with thirty-one dates in total. It would be the closest Caroline got – so far – to that career as a professional dancer in a West End show she had dreamed of as a child. Ultimately, Scott Mills and Simon Webbe were signed up too. It was to provide her with something to look forward to, a distraction in times that were to become very difficult.

For behind the scenes, all was not well. There has long been talk of the '*Strictly* curse', based on the fact that so many relationships featuring contestants seemed to end following their appearances on the show. This was, perhaps, not so much a curse as an inevitability – it's the sort of thing that is likely to happen when you get young and attractive people spending hours in each other's company, hours spent in close physical contact, at that. For the same reason, there had been quite a few relationships that had actually started on *Strictly*. But Caroline had not been concerned about it when she went on the show.

'Jack's been completely fine about the whole curse thing,' she told the *Mirror*. 'He hasn't once been worried. If anything, doing the show has made our relationship better than ever because I'm happier. It's made me a happier person. It's something so different to what I'm used to that he says it's brought out a nicer side of me – not that I was bad before. But whatever *Strictly* does to other couples, for whatever reason, it's done the opposite to us.'

Alas, as the show neared the semi-final, there were reports that Caroline had been seen 'distraught' backstage and that the pair had split. In the usual run of things it would be that a *Strictly* contestant or professional dancer had run off with someone else on the show. This time around, it was Jack who had met someone new. A source told the *Sun*, 'It came to a natural end and it was mutual,' but that was by no means the full story. Jack, it seems, had been showing an interest in *Glee* star Dianna Agron, who had starred in Sam Smith's 'I'm Not the Only One' video.

Jack was in the USA for the video when he was pictured with the actress, and this was how Caroline first got to know about it. She was devastated and furious and took to Twitter, as she so often did these days: 'Easing your guilt?' she tweeted in reply to a tweet of his own, in which he urged people to vote for her on *Strictly*. 'Fill yourself with Glee, Jack.' This was soon deleted and replaced with the poignant, 'It's not bad to be sad.' She was sad, though, very, and it was to be quite a while before she fully recovered.

But the show must go on. Caroline refused to comment publicly; putting a brave face on it, she and Pasha danced towards the final and she also took part in an Alan Carr new year special. She was pictured out in miniskirts showing off her toned legs and, back at *Strictly*, managed that semi-final score of a perfect forty – including a ten from Craig Revel Horwood, a score which wasn't very often given. 'I think it was the greatest moment of my life,' said Caroline. 'My biggest achievement.'

Pasha was stunned too: 'I was surprised by the forty, actually,' he said. 'It was amazing but at the same time, like, "Really?" It just happened but it was a lot of fun.'

Of course, dancing is physical exercise – it is recommended both for heartbreak and depression, and while her public knew that Caroline had problems with the former, it was still totally unknown that she also had serious issues with the latter. The break-up did not help. It cut her to the core, far more than people realised, but *Strictly* did at least take her mind off it temporarily. 'It's changed my mind about everything I want to do,' said Caroline of the programme. 'It's completely opened up my mind to different things I want to try – it's given me a massive boost in confidence and it's made me feel very positive. I just know there's other things I

can do now. It shows you can put your mind to anything …
It releases all these endorphins that I never knew were there,
naturally, and you just come out on a high every day.'

Better still, it was beating her former employer in the
ratings although Caroline, wisely, wasn't gloating. 'I had three
brilliant years on *The X Factor* and it was one of the best jobs
I've ever had,' she said. '*Strictly* is completely different, it's a
whole different show – I'm dancing, it's not presenting. But
this is one of the best things I've done – ever.' And of course
the viewers warmed to all this positivity: Caroline's warmth
and enthusiasm came across on the screen. She really was
putting her all into those dances, chanelling her energy and
clearly loving every moment of the performances. She had,
after all, wanted to be a professional dancer as a child.

But the split had taken its toll and nothing, not even the
joy of doing *Strictly*, could make up for that. 'She has really
been suffering but is putting on a brave face for the cameras,'
a source told the *Sun*. 'It was hard for her to find out about
Dianna – especially as Jack was the man she thought she was
going to marry. Their split was a painful decision and has
put a massive strain on the whole *Strictly* process for her. But
having to concentrate on eight-hour rehearsals every day is
helping take her mind off things. She is just getting on with
it, like everyone else who has been in the same situation has
had to do.'

Caroline later revealed that Pasha knew about the turmoil
she was going through and they directed it into that last,
glorious dance. 'We had a very emotional week as we practised
it, knowing our time together was coming to an end,' she
told the *Birmingham Mail*. 'And dancing it in the final was so
emotional. Pasha taught me how to express my emotions
through dance. I put a year's worth of all these emotions into

a minute-and-a-half of dance. It was so therapeutic. The showdance is my favourite of all the ones we danced during the competition. Pasha spent so long choreographing it – it was like doing a ballet.'

And so came the big win, the glitter trophy and praise all round. 'My heart has melted,' said Craig, adding for good measure she was, 'absolutely phenomenal'. All of the judges fell over themselves with praise. Darcey called her 'the perfect naughty flapper', Bruno named her his 'golden sex goddess … The Earth was moving. I'm still basking in the afterglow.' The showdance, featuring a wind machine, was 'like watching a contemporary ballet,' said Darcey. Len added, 'You don't need wind machines, you've got huge fans up here.'

Even the bookies got in on the act: they cut Caroline's odds to 1–4, while a Coral spokeswoman said, 'After weeks of getting off the hook, we've finally got our fingers burnt. Caroline Flack was backed off the boards tonight and has left us facing a hefty Christmas payout.'

'I could not imagine a better partner,' added Pasha. There was happiness on the screen, if not in real life.

Unsurprisingly, there was an extremely emotional Caroline. 'This is the best feeling in the whole world. This has been the best experience of my whole life,' she told her fellow competitors. 'I've been so lucky to get to know you … This has been a complete bonding experience for everybody. Thank you so much for voting as well, it's been so lovely.' The viewers were delighted, Twitter was full of messages of praise and Caroline partied the night away at the after-show bash.

She also took to Twitter: 'Last night the best night of my life … A real incredible group of people whom yesterday were a complete joy to be dancing with xx And THANK YOU for supporting me and Pasha throughout the series … What a night … I can't even lift my head let alone the glitterball :)' And on the subject of the mighty glitterball, she said, 'They give you a mini-glitterball to keep, rather than the big trophy and I've been carrying that round with me. I don't want to put it down! And I'm going to see if I can buy my Union Jack dress in which I jived to "Crocodile Rock", because I'd love to wear that at parties.'

As for the trophy itself, matters went a bit haywire in the aftermath of the show. 'I went with my friends to a random house party in west London after the *Strictly* final – we stayed until 7 a.m. and got so drunk I left my glitterball there,' she told *Radio Times* a few months later. 'The next day, I had to go and knock on this man's door and say, "Hi – I think I left my glitterball in your house … "' As for displaying it later: 'I actually gave it to my niece to take into school for a show-and-tell, and she never gave it back. It's probably still in her bedroom.'

There was talk about roles in the West End in the wake of the victory, about the millions Caroline could make if she played her cards carefully, the opportunities ahead. She was pretty overwhelmed: 'I'd love to do something musical,' she said. '*Strictly* has been a real outlet for me. You can't feel unhappy when you are dancing. It's impossible. It's amazing to end the year on a high. It has been an interesting year and very testing in a lot of ways.'

More than she was letting on. As revealed at the start of this book, she actually awoke the morning after *Strictly* in despair following the end of the relationship and it was to be a long time before she was properly over it. She certainly tried: she headed off to Jamaica over the new year with her friend Lou Teasdale – who just happened to be Harry Styles's hair stylist – and put on a good show in public, still the laughing, tanned tomboy so many loved. But the saga with Jack was to continue for a while yet.

The pair did in fact have a brief reconciliation the following year and were spotted at festivals together – whatever the link with Dianna had been, it was over – but the relationship didn't last. This time the split was permanent and the hurt was to be severe. '@jackb_street dear you. Tiny little man. You'll never change for anyone. But good luck with that,' tweeted Caroline, who later called him evil. She later deleted the tweet but the hurt lingered on. The following year, on the day she was to hit the red carpet for the launch of *The X Factor*, of which more anon, Sam Smith somewhat tactlessly posted a picture of Jack cosying up to a new woman, prompting another emotional outburst from Caroline on Instagram. Her post showed her holding a disco ball captioned, 'When someone who knows you more than anyone ruins the biggest day of your life' (this was assumed to refer to Jack rather than Sam).

It is a cliché, but the sequins couldn't mask the heartache. 'Caroline is heartbroken to see him move on so fast,' a source told the *Mirror*. 'She thought they could make a go of it the second time. Clearly, it's over now. This break-up has been even more acrimonious than the last. And the timing of him going public with a new girlfriend couldn't have been worse.'

The repercussions of this actually lasted for years. Like many people who struggled with depression, Caroline already had a tendency to drink too much and Jack-related matters were to make it worse. Some time later Caroline bumped into Jack at Glastonbury with his girlfriend, the model Emma Champtaloup. It knocked her for six.

'Caroline started drinking and just didn't stop after she saw Jack and Emma,' a friend told *Now*. 'She'd worked so hard on getting over him and was really turning a corner but it seemed to really knock her off balance. She was arguing with the people closest to her and even started blocking people on all her social networks if she saw they'd been talking to Jack.' It was a wound that went deep.

8

STRICTLY COME TOURING

It had been a very unhappy time personally, but for January 2015 at least, the Strictly Come Dancing tour would keep Caroline occupied.

It was also a helpful transition away from the show. The *Strictly* experience was so all-consuming that it almost took over the whole of a contestant's life, what with eight hours training a day on top of the recording itself, and to go from that to nothing would have been a shock. But the downside of touring was that Caroline was on the road for weeks, away from her nearest and dearest, at a time when she was vulnerable and despondent. All the work in the world could not make up for that, and that unhappiness was to keep gnawing away at her. Caroline was in her mid-thirties now and, while that was no age for a woman these days, at the same time she had made no secret of her wish to get married and settle down. That looked further away than ever. And there was that ongoing vulnerability. Caroline was nothing like as tough as she looked.

A stomach bug kept her from the photo call for the launch of the tour, but audiences were assured she would be OK for the first night. And then it was on with the show: she missed dancing with Pasha, but at the same time Caroline was in many ways looking forward to it. Rehearsals were soon underway, without Frankie – she dropped out as she was pregnant – but the dancers were preparing for the week ahead. Caroline was ever the trouper: there was no sign in public whatsoever of the inner turmoil she was experiencing as the tour got underway. She was partnered with Tristan MacManus, the Irish dancer who was a stalwart not only of *Strictly* but also other shows such as *Dancing With the Stars*. Caroline looked sensational as she kicked off the first night at the Barclaycard Arena, Birmingham, dressed in a multi-coloured top that highlighted her figure, and grey, high-waisted shorts that showed off her legs – her trademark look. These were later swapped for a plunging silver dress in her ballroom routine and a fringed number with gold tassels. The other participants were equally spangly and were greeted with uproarious applause.

Caroline really was a pro: night after night she put a beaming face on display, showed formidable energy on the stage and demonstrated her determination to dance away her troubles. But away from the spotlight, things were far more bleak. In public, Caroline could not have been more positive. '*Strictly* coming to an end on TV is a big comedown, so going on tour is a nice way to wean us off. The *Strictly* bubble hasn't burst quite yet!' she told the *Birmingham Mail*. 'I had a lovely, relaxing new year in Jamaica and I think 2015 is going to be an interesting year and a lot of fun. *Strictly* is definitely life-changing and I hope it can open another pathway for me, career-wise. Maybe something a bit more musical. I haven't been into the office yet so I haven't heard what offers have come in. I would love to do a West End show, but that's just a big dream at the moment.' One which was going to come true.

And there were also her new year resolutions, with Caroline – perhaps unwittingly – revealing that she was really drinking too much. Personal unhappiness aside, she was also experiencing the pressures of success: more in the public eye than she ever had been before, Caroline needed to keep going at the same pace and this was not always easy. But she laughed it off. One of her resolutions was 'to drink more water, I don't drink nearly enough. I'll still drink alcohol, but my aim is to have one glass of water for every glass of booze,' she said. 'I'm a massive foodie and I hate diets, but I might have to rein it in a little bit after the tour. Using up so many calories in training, I could eat whatever I liked. That meant I didn't lose any weight but I did tone up. Without all the exercise, I can't eat as much!' She was making light of it all but the relationship between depression and alcohol is well established and it was doing little for her mental state.

In the meantime, more details of Caroline's dancing past were being revealed, when veteran choreographer and past *Strictly* judge Arlene Phillips announced that she had actually once seen Caroline at an audition: it was only now that it was really beginning to emerge that there should be no surprise at Caroline's dancing ability, because she'd trained for years. 'I know Caroline as a dancer because years and years ago she auditioned for *Starlight Express*. And she didn't get in!' Arlene, who had done the choreography for the show told Daily Star Online. ' Listen, she's a really lovely dancer, beautiful. She definitely has a career in it – you bet ya. I'd cast her in a show. I'd hire her in a heartbeat. How well she sings, I don't know yet. The right role would really depend on her voice because most people in musical theatre have to be able to sing, but she is sassy and charming, and she really can dance. It's exciting. I want to hear her sing and I will find a show for her.' Shows were eventually to come, but not for a few years yet.

The *Strictly* tour moved off around the country but, while the exercise was undoubtedly good for Caroline's state of mind, she wasn't always onstage, pulling out of a show in Nottingham saying that she was unwell and had to get better. Tellingly, there was a groan from the audience when it was announced she wouldn't be appearing as Caroline was one of the most popular elements of the show. But while the fans couldn't have had a clue about Caroline's true state of mind, the other dancers did. After Caroline's death, Kristina Rihanoff, who was also on the tour, appeared on *Good Morning Britain* to say there were clear signs that Caroline had been struggling. She was 'bubbly and sweet' said Kristina, but had 'insecurities and vulnerabilities'. Could anyone have helped? Probably not. In the wake of Caroline's death there would be a palpable desire to lay the blame somewhere but, once depression really takes hold of someone, it can be extremely difficult to shift. And at the time, no one realised the extent of the trouble she was having.

'During the show she always appeared bubbly, sweet and happy. Everyone loved working with her. She always had a smile on her face,' Kristina said. 'When you're touring especially, which we did after *Strictly Come Dancing*, there were many demons. A couple of times she missed going on stage because she was battling inner demons. We sat down and spoke and you could see she had a lot of insecurities and vulnerability that wasn't known to the public. It's sad what happened. There should have been a life coach or someone to help. She couldn't see a way out.' It was at this time that

Caroline also started to take antidepressants, something she was very open about a few years down the line, although it was largely kept behind the scenes to begin with.

Ironically, given her self-doubts, Caroline was increasingly cited as one of the sexiest women in the world. In 2015, she was voted fifth-sexiest by listeners to Heart radio, having not been on the list at all the previous year and coming in at seventieth in 2013 and forty-eighth in 2012. This was partly due to her increased profile, of course: the impact of *Strictly* on her profile had been huge and people were far more aware of her than they had been previously. But this was not a one-off. Caroline was also asked to model for Naomi Campbell's Fashion For Relief show, which was to raise funds to combat the Ebola crisis in West Africa. She carried it off with aplomb, as she strutted down the runway at Somerset House; she was wearing a bow-embellished prom dress, topped by a crown-shaped hat with netting across her face. Another of the models was her old friend Pixie Lott.

Home for Caroline was by now in north-east London, a space she shared with her cat Waffle – she was so attached to the animal that she even got a tattoo of her pet. But behind the scenes the pressure really was beginning to tell. Caroline was open about the fact that her 'ditzy' persona could not continue in television forever, on top of which the split with Jack really continued to rankle. 'It was such a bittersweet moment of winning the show, but also that feeling of, "Could you not have just waited three more weeks and then broken up with me?!"' she said in an interview with *Red* magazine. 'When I woke up the next day it was like someone had put clingfilm over my bed and I couldn't get up. I'd never felt like that before, numb, like everything had come to an end. And everyone was going, "Carrie! You've just won *Strictly*!"

and I was like, "I know but I just don't feel happy." I was heartbroken. At the time it's all-consuming, but it gets better.' She was now dating, she said, although it was 'quite weird. It gives you lots of anecdotes and stories to tell your friends. I can't really do Tinder, I might get some strange people. I've had a few stalkers in my time so it might be best not to.' She didn't have a particular type of person in mind. 'I don't care what they do – they could work in a shoe shop, they could work in politics, you can't help who you fall in love with, it just happens. I usually meet people through friends or through work. So ... anyone got any mates?!' She was linked to Matt Healy, the twenty-something frontman of The 1975, when the two were seen cuddling at a Brits after-party in March, but nothing more came of it.

Indeed, it seemed her inner turmoil was still very much in evidence. There was that brief reunion with Jack, but if anything that just seemed to make her more unhappy. 'Drunk texting is the worst, isn't it?' she said in one interview. 'Oh God, and you wake up in the morning like, "Right, if I delete it, it didn't happen – get on with your day."' She was also deleting tweets and her worrying obsession with social media continued. On the one hand, she was aware that social media did not tell a person's full story, but on the other she was affected by what she read and saw. Friends would relate that she would spend hours going over what was said about her on social media and, inevitably, not all of it was kind. Quite the opposite. Trolling had become quite the thing by now and, as the culprits were hiding behind their online personas of anonymity, Caroline was forced to see some pretty unpleasant remarks about herself. And, given that she was nothing like as thick-skinned as some took her to be, this was bound to have an effect.

As usual, however, she tried to put a brave face on it. 'It's all just pretend,' she told *Red*. 'You can have the saddest day you've ever had and then put a picture of yourself going [mimes a star jump and a ridiculous grin] and everyone thinks, "Oh, she's got such a good life." I never take them [the comments] to heart, they're just loonies. I'm immune to it. You realise they're just unhappy people who write nasty things. [But] there's a lot of pressure with young girls and Instagram to do the right angles; look thin – look like they're pop stars. And my ten-year-old niece, Willow, is now on Instagram and I just feel like she's too young. Without offending anybody, there are these Instagram idols out there who aren't like the idols we had as kids.'

And then there were hurtful comments relating to her appearance – which every woman in the public eye must put up with – but were not easy to read. For example, there was the magazine that published a story saying she looked as if she were expecting a child. 'I try not to engage but, now and again, if they catch me in the wrong mood … Do not say I look pregnant,' said Caroline. 'You don't know what I was doing the day before or after. Maybe I am pregnant or maybe I *was* pregnant. Things like that really piss me off. You know nothing about what's going on in my life. I know I shouldn't rise to it but I'm impulsive. Then I'll call my twin sister Jo and say, "Oh my God, I've done something bad but I couldn't help it!" She says, "You know what, Carrie? You're just human."'

She was indeed but, as ever with Caroline, although her personal life was difficult, she was managing to get on as well as possible. That year, rumours surfaced in the spring that she was in the running to be the presenter of *The X Factor*, a sweet prospect, given that losing *The Xtra Factor* had caused some upset. And then she was linked to a new show, with the intriguing title *Love Island*, of which much, much more anon. And she also released her autobiography, *Storm in a C Cup*, in which she was far more open than many had expected about the men in her life, especially the two Harrys. Had she warned the men that the book was about to appear? Yes, she announced on television – although she didn't reveal what their responses were. But the book also revealed that, while she might have had an idyllic childhood in rural Norfolk, she had fought long and hard for her television career and that there was a dark side to her life that no one could have dreamed of before. But for now Caroline was battling on. She had a new show to do.

9

THE X FACTOR?

As it turned out, Caroline had been very wise indeed to keep up good relations with Simon Cowell. For it was in 2015 that she was to take on two of the biggest names in television, one, it must be said, rather more successfully than the other. She had already started on *Love Island* when she became involved with *The X Factor* – this time not on its little sister sidekick show, but the main gig itself.

The X Factor took place in five stages: producer auditions, judge auditions, boot camp, judges' houses and live shows. The roster of judges changed year by year. Its first presenter had been the journalist and presenter (and one-time editor of *Smash Hits*) Kate Thornton but, from 2007 it had been in the hands of British-Irish television presenter Dermot O'Leary. In 2015, to everyone's astonishment, he said that he'd had enough. Many reasons were cited at the time, not least the nine months of the year it dominated his life, although Dermot himself later revealed he'd actually had enough of problems involving his contract. 'At the end of every series you were left not knowing if your contract was going to be renewed,' he told Entertainment Daily. 'I remember being in Austin, Texas, and still not having heard whether I was going to be doing *The X Factor*, which would have started in a matter of weeks. I made a call to ITV and was told I might be doing it, but I might not. I'd done eight years there very successfully and I thought, I'm not playing these games any more. So I called ITV and told them to count me out.'

Who would replace him at such short notice? The role was much harder than it looked: it took a presenter who could think on their feet and keep a light touch to the proceedings. All the usual suspects were in the frame – Sarah-Jane Crawford, who had succeeded Caroline at *The Xtra Factor*, ex-*X Factor* singer Marvin Humes, at that stage hosting *The Voice*, *American Idol* host Ryan Seacrest or perhaps presenter Emma Willis? But the choice seemed obvious: who better to step into *The X Factor* shoes than the people who had been looking after the secondary version? Step forward Caroline Flack and Olly Murs.

The duo – the first couple to present the show – duly issued a statement. 'I'm incredibly excited and proud to be returning to *The X Factor* alongside Caroline,' said Olly. 'I love the show and it kickstarted my career in music, which has given me the opportunity to do what I love. I already have the best job in the world and it's about to get better – I can't wait to get started and be part of finding some amazing new talent!'

'I'm beyond excited about presenting *The X Factor* with Olly,' Caroline said. 'To have the privilege of doing this with someone who makes me laugh out loud is a massive bonus!' And displaying that tact she had always previously shown, she also had praise for the departing Dermot. 'I'm also incredibly lucky to have the best tips and support from my showbiz big brother Dermot,' she added. 'I'm not sure how I can live up to his long-term residency but I know I can't let him down!'

Caroline had, in fact, already started her next job, but the producers of *The X Factor* were so determined to snap her up that they were prepared to work around the two roles. 'I had already agreed to do *Love Island* when they approached me and I thought, Uh-oh, they're going to clash – is there any way I could do both? But they wiggled around the schedules so I could,' she told *Radio Times*. She made for a pretty obvious choice: Caroline's increased profile after the stint on *Strictly*, her on-screen chemistry with Olly and her own aptitude at hoofing all played in her favour. In the event, however, matters didn't go entirely according to plan. There were other changes elsewhere: Louis Walsh stepped down from the show after eleven years and Nick Grimshaw and Rita Ora, who had been a coach on *The Voice*, arrived as judges.

Caroline and Olly, who were doing everything together now (almost), gave a joint interview to the *Sun*, in which they revealed how Simon had persuaded the two of them to take on the show. 'He asked if I wanted a curry and I said, "I love curry,"' Olly revealed. 'So I go round to his house and he has all these amazing curries that have been made in his kitchen. There was a spicy chicken curry and a milder one, and all these dishes of chutneys and papadums and naan bread – a proper feast. But at his end of the table there was this huge bowl of shepherd's pie. He said, "I decided I didn't want curry in the end, so I'm having shepherd's pie. But I know you wanted curry." So I had to work my way through all these different curries and we had a good chat about the show.'

Caroline didn't get quite such lavish treatment and initially didn't realise quite what was on the – metaphorical – table.

'I definitely didn't get fed,' she said. 'I had one glass of wine, that was it. I went to see Simon in January and we talked about *Strictly* and all sorts of things. But nothing was really mentioned about me doing *X Factor*. It was a nice catch-up because I hadn't seen him for ages. I thought he was going to offer me some kind of big new show. Then nothing happened and I was like, "Oh … ' Then, when Dermot said he was leaving, things happened quite quickly.'

Rightly or wrongly, there was the perception that *The X Factor* had gone a little stale and needed to be perked up. Would the two new presenters do the trick? Tactful Caroline was wary about criticising the show per se, which would have upset everyone involved, including the people who had just given her a job, and so instead talked about the interplay between her and Olly. Of their double act, she said 'We've got to change it slightly. We've got to take away the silliness a little bit. We can bring fun to it and bring excitement but it's got to be about the contestants and their relationship with the judges and of course the audience and their voting. He's going to have a nice relationship with Simon because they know each other really well.'

She was also happy to defend her new gig from the naysayers, of which there were a few. 'I think *X Factor* is offering opportunity to people who don't have that opportunity anywhere else,' she said. 'You could look at that programme and find a million negative things but you can also find a million positive things. Some people just love that negative vibe. I guess a lot of people say it's changed the music industry a lot, people say it's taken advantage of people and putting their life onto TV and using that. But it is a TV show at the end of the day. It's a really entertaining TV show and it's only giving people an opportunity. That's all it's doing.'

The first round kicked off at EventCity, Manchester, Caroline resplendent in in a black playsuit, matching wedges and a silver belt. 'Hello Manchester!' she tweeted, as she was now spending a huge amount of time on the social media site, before exchanging banter with Olly. The tweeting certainly was constant: after seeing a show with her childhood heroine Kylie Minogue, Caroline posted her approval; when some trolls told her she looked pregnant, she told them to F-off. The trolls were an unpleasant constant in the background, all the more so as Caroline was now such a high-profile figure and they could be extremely abusive.

'I had a little wobbly when I broke down in tears after the second live show,' she told the *Daily Star*. 'I got a message from a friend asking if I was OK because of all the abuse I was getting online. I then looked and it was really personal and horrible. It's the personal things that hurt. As a female they pick on everything. Your hair, your dress, your weight. I did have a cry and Olly gave me a big hug, bless him. I've had to learn to have thick skin, but it doesn't mean you can handle every bullet that is fired at you. Some of it really hurts.' Despite what she told the paper, poor Caroline had not developed that thick a skin, though, and continued to be deeply wounded by the slights. (Cheryl, who was a judge, also got trolled, in her case on the grounds she was too slim.)

Upheaval continued. Rehearsals were postponed at one point when Simon Cowell lost his mother, to whom he was extremely close. Voiceover legend Peter Dickson quit. Caroline herself was a bundle of nerves: on the first day of filming, she asked Simon if he thought all the talent in the UK had been exhausted and he told her that was a stupid question and walked away. But she also felt that Simon had enormous presence, able to change the atmosphere of a room simply by entering.

The actual broadcasts began in September 2015 – taking place some three weeks after Caroline's final split from Jack. The show's great competition, ironically, came from *Strictly*, where Caroline had been only the previous year. The judges were soon allocated: Simon for the over-twenty-fives, Cheryl for the groups, Rita Ora the girls and Nick Grimshaw the boys.

Caroline took a short break to appear at the *Strictly* launch, where she was reunited with Pasha to perform the winner's dance, which she carried off with aplomb in a scarlet mini-dress. She returned to *The X Factor* to find that all was not going as smoothly as planned. Ratings were down on the previous year, with no one entirely sure why (although there was plenty of speculation) and no one seemed to quite know what to do to resolve the situation. Caroline and Olly gamely struggled on, flirting as much as ever in the course of the relationship that never was. At one typical point, Caroline said, 'I'm completely professional. When I'm standing next to Olly it's hard to concentrate on any other man.' She also confessed that her mother would love her to marry Olly. There may have been chemistry between Caroline and Olly, but they weren't really getting to show it, as some people pointed to the fact that Caroline was getting very little screen time.

More general criticism of the direction of the show came from high-profile figures, including Graham Norton. 'I haven't watched *X Factor* the past few years because it just seems so long now – it's endless,' he told the *Mirror*. 'Also, the people aren't very good, so to all the judges' comments of, "I'd buy your album tomorrow," you think, You're never having an album. You wouldn't throw 50p at them if they were busking in the tube. I think it's lost its credibility.' None of this criticism was aimed directly at Caroline, but for someone with low self-esteem anyway, it can't have been pleasant to be in the middle of this particular storm. Former judge Louis Walsh weighed in on his own replacement: 'I'm not sure about Grimshaw,' he said. 'I haven't seen much of him. People don't like change and I think they miss Dermot and maybe some people miss me.'

As the series progressed, interest in Caroline's love life remained as strong as ever, not least as she was now involved in *Love Island*. Now that she and Jack were definitely through, could there be anyone else? 'I've always got time for a relationship,' she said in an interview with *Cosmopolitan*. 'If you like someone, even if its 2 a.m. and you've just finished work, then you get that lovely feeling where you want to see them for an hour. I've always got time for that. I could use Tinder, but I'm quite traditional when it comes to meeting people. It's a chemistry thing – you feel it, or you don't.' And people were still going on about Prince Harry. 'Being asked about the Harry thing doesn't bug me,' said a sporting Caroline. 'People are interested in those sort of things because they're in the public domain. You learn to laugh it off. It's funny, it's not serious.'

In the autumn, Caroline did a series of interviews and, reading between the lines, it seems clear that there was still a lot of personal anguish going on. 'Heartbreak is just a very lonely place to be,' she told the *Sun*. 'You're on your own and there's no cure, so it's something you have to solve on your own. I'd love there to be a pill you can take for heartbreak ... dating is a funny thing, innit? When you're single, people assume that you don't want to be. And, actually, being single and happy is often the best place to be. Happiness isn't about being with someone else and some of the happiest times in my life have been on my own. I don't need to be with someone, and if I did then I would be.' The second break from Jack was still recent at that point and Caroline said she was dating 'here and there' but she didn't sound particularly happy with her lot.

She also made the news when she accidentally published a selfie that revealed rather more than it was meant to and after that she took a short break in Portugal while debate continued over the state of the show. As the boot camp stage of *X Factor* got underway, Olly broke up with his girlfriend, leading to intensive speculation that he and Caroline would get together. It was not going to happen, as the pair constantly told the fans. Not that that stopped the Twitter brigade: some felt compelled to warn Caroline to stay away from Olly, despite the fact that she had repeatedly said she wasn't interested in him. They lashed out from under the cloak of anonymity. As Caroline suffered the online crowd continued with their bullying behaviour. No one knew the toll it took.

There was more bad news. Caroline injured her arm in a bike accident as the live shows approached and her absence from the screen – at one point, also due to her filming *Strictly* – continued to be the subject of comment. And even when she was on screen there was no respite: both professional critics and the Twitter mob agreed that she and Olly just were not managing to pull off the live shows. *Strictly* was pulling in over ten million in the ratings, while *The X Factor* was managing only just over five: some people were calling for the return of Dermot O'Leary.

Caroline appeared on *This Morning* and was directly asked about the failing show: 'Everyone has an opinion,' she replied. 'They all comment on what you wear, how you talk and how you breathe, especially on a show like *The X Factor*. You have to have a thick skin.' But, of course, she didn't, and the viewer reaction to the judges' houses element was extremely negative, with it being labelled 'shambolic'. And, of course, with so much negativity in the air, tension went up, which in turn affected the proceedings. The magic that Caroline and Ollie had managed to create before just wasn't there. Meanwhile, Simon himself recognised that the live performances hadn't worked and was talking about axing the judges' houses the following year. The biggest problem was that the acts had been forced to beg to stay on the show.

'As far as this week goes, it's back to basics,' Simon told the *Mirror* after the event. 'Last weekend I was like, "Woah". It was too crazy. I had just been back a day from America and was jet-lagged. I walked on to the show and hadn't a clue what was going on half the time. Then I realised, "Oh my God, they've been asked to beg – I can't do this." So we stopped it on day two. Uncomfortable? It was horrific, so that's scrapped one hundred per cent. It was shambolic. It certainly gave me a kick up the arse and made me look at this week. I don't know whose decision it was and I'm not blaming anyone. It just wasn't right. The groups went up and suddenly were like begging.

'I said, "Look, I had no idea this was going on but please don't beg – just make a clear point why you should be there." Then at the end of the show I said, "We can't do that."' Simon also commented that Caroline and Olly had been 'thrown into the lions' den a little bit'. Many others were not so kind.

Caroline was in the wars: straight after hurting her arm, she came down with the flu, threatening to cause a problem in presenting the live shows. In the event, she recovered in time, but the pressure was on both her and Olly, as the man himself admitted. 'I'm massively sh***ing myself,' he said to Express.co.uk. 'I'm quite a confident character and, obviously, I always get to perform in front of people and sing but, on this occasion, I'm going to be talking to people and hosting the show so it's a bit different to what I'm used to. If I get nervous I can just sing. Maybe that's what I'll do. Me and Caroline have worked together a lot so for us both we're both there, we can both talk to each other and we're used to being together on TV so it's great.'

But a lot was riding on how the *X Factor* performed from this point onwards, with yet more pressure exerted on the duo when it was suggested that the live shows gave them a chance to 'prove' themselves. Someone who understood this pressure was Dermot O'Leary, who tweeted to wish the two of them good luck just before the live proceedings kicked off, but although they acquitted themselves perfectly well, viewers were now openly calling for the return of the former presenter, creating a hashtag #bringbackdermot.

'Can you double eliminate Olly Murs and Caroline Flack?,' asked one. 'They are worse than the #XFactor Group Song.'

'Never seen anything more painful than Olly Murs and Caroline Flack trying to host @TheXFactor,' added another.

Caroline laughed it off. 'Thanks for all your lovely tweets from the weekend!' she replied. 'I am having a blast presenting the show!'

What was going wrong? Both Olly and Caroline were going through a difficult phase in their love lives, both having split from their partners, which would have an effect on anyone's state of mind. But the two of them were both professionals, they sparked off one another and they had had a hugely successful partnership for years. It was suggested that there had been too many changes to the show to go down well with the public and it was widely acknowledged that the chaos surrounding the judges' houses was not actually their fault. It was further suggested that they were two people doing one person's job. And the public had had eight years of Dermot and were used to him: it might simply have been a reaction to unwanted change. But a vicious circle can become exactly that: if people lose their nerve, they continue to perform under par, which just makes matters worse. And Caroline and Olly would not have been human if they had not been demoralised by the whole experience.

Indeed, it appeared to get too much for Olly at one point. 'It's cynical,' he told BBC radio's *Newsbeat* of the online abuse. 'They're not even fans of the show ... They just want to slag the show off for some reason. When you think about it, we've got eleven amazing contestants this year and – obviously, me being an ex-contestant – that's where the focus should be. And that's where it used to be. For some reason, over the last four or five years, people have decided to go against everything else apart from looking at the talent.'

But they struggled on. Personally, Caroline was linked to another younger man, Harry's One Direction colleague Niall Horan (in actual fact, it was nothing more than a bit of flirting) and was pictured out on the town, as lively as ever. Soon enough, the second live show approached and, this time round, Caroline and Olly played up to the will they/won't they rumours by appearing to kiss as they left the stage, before pulling back just in time. Caroline also gave an interview to the *Daily Mail* that hinted there was more to the relationship than they had so far confessed: 'Me and Olly have a lovely relationship,' she says. 'It's a weird chemistry. We have this innate understanding of one another – we don't fancy each other and yet we don't not fancy each other. We're not girlfriend and boyfriend, yet we're not totally platonic either.'

Her thirty-sixth birthday approached: Olly tweeted his congrats and said he couldn't wait for a night on the tiles; this duly happened when the two were pictured after the live show. Olly first shared a selfie from the car with Caroline and a group of friends; the next day he posted a snap of Caroline with a chocolate cake, saying, 'Happy birthday to my co-host & best bud @carolineflack1 love ya long time.' He then, however, went on to give an interview in which he said there was absolutely no romance.

One Direction appeared on the show: viewers said that Caroline kept her distance (had she not done, that would almost certainly have resulted in even more comment). In truth, whatever she did would have been talked about. Olly was criticised for not including Harry in the interview that followed, until he was pushed into it by the audience's response.

Then there was a really embarrassing moment, as Olly consoled Monica Michael for having been voted off before her name was actually announced. This caused uproar and prompted claims that the show had been fixed: there was talk of sacking Olly (it didn't happen) and Monica herself revealed that Olly had been devastated backstage. In time-honoured fashion his thoughts were tweeted: 'I apologise to everyone tonight I made a massive f**k up at the end. It was so tense!! I'm still learning & hope that never happens again!' Everyone hoped it would never happen again. He pulled out of a private DVD screening in response, it was said, to terrorist attacks unfolding in Paris that weekend, while none other than Dermot tweeted his support. Caroline put a picture of the two of them hugging on Instagram, captioned, 'Life is better with you in it, buddy.'

But Twitter lit up in the wake of the mistake: One user said, 'Harry Styles watches on as Olly Murs begs at the feet of Simon Cowell to keep his job … "You alright down there, Olly?"' Another commented, 'Beginning of the end of Olly Murs career tonight … . Oops.' The tweets continued: 'The next person leaving xfactor is Olly Murs. Deadlock.' And another posted: 'Olly Murs is as bad at presenting as he is at singing. How utterly embarrassing. He can barely pronounce most words but that?!'

Abject apologies continued to be issued from *The X Factor* as the calls for Dermot to return grew louder. It was left to Caroline to address them. 'I just think the online critics are a tough crowd, aren't they?' she said at an ITV gala. 'He made a mistake, I make loads of mistakes, but you put it behind you and carry on. We might mention it this weekend as a joke, I might be sending it to deadlock if it does. Just don't do it again, Olly!' Simon had been 'really lovely' about it, she said. 'He's a great boss. He's not the kind of guy that would be, "You shouldn't have done that," he's like, "You live and you learn."'

She also talked about the amount of criticism she and Olly had to endure as a pair presented *X Factor*. 'He was really sad. No one wants to see a sad Olly. I really felt for him. He was kicking himself. It's hard for us to do the show each week when people have been criticising us. But we're a team and you can't think about that when you're presenting the show.'

Olly, while penitent, was also clearly getting tired of the fuss. 'I think you need to put it in perspective with everything that's going on in the world,' he said at the same gala. 'At the end of the day, I made a single mistake at a critical point in *X Factor*, which was massively blown out of proportion. I had no idea Monica was going until I got the envelope. And it was just a really awkward moment for me because I made a stupid mistake. I was expecting a telling off [from Simon] if I'm honest but I didn't get one which was nice. I saw everyone after, I saw Monica, I saw all the judges and said I was so sorry and let myself down.' In other words – enough!

But people still weighed in. When Louis Walsh claimed that Olly was a 'pop star pretending to be a presenter,' Simon Cowell himself was prompted to wade in.

'There were a lot of people screaming in his ears, they were trying to get him to clarify something,' he told the *Mirror*. 'Anyone in that situation is going to screw up. I think the way he handled it was great, it's part of his charm. I think every week he's getting better and better. People have got to get used to it but he's got a massive future ahead of him, one hundred per cent he's still got my support.' There were reports that Simon had told Olly and Caroline not to check their phones when they were backstage, because he didn't want them to be upset by the snide remarks.

The finals continued. In late November the show took 'heartbreak' as its theme: this was on Caroline's suggestion. Simon loved it and dedicated it to her. She took it well: 'I sent a text to Simon and said we should do heartbreak week,' she told the *Daily Star*. 'He texted back and said, "Great idea Caroline, I love it." Then two days later he texted me saying, "We are doing it next week and I'm dedicating it to you. I'm sure you know lots of angry songs." He kept walking past with different angry songs and said, "We'll dedicate each song to one of your relationships."'

On the night in question, Olly and Caroline played up her influence in the genre of the week: Olly showered his friend with kisses and said, 'It's love … and heartbreak. Love, because Caroline, I'll always love you.'

'And heartbreak,' said Caroline, 'because, Olly, it's never gonna happen. Oh, sorry!'

Olly dropped to his knees front of her. The judges started laughing. It was all very good-humoured, but no one was claiming that Caroline and Olly's stint on the show had been an unmitigated success. Olly began dropping hints that he might quit to focus on his pop career; Caroline remarked that the show was so all-consuming and there was no downtime. She loved it, she said, but there was a hint of exhaustion.

In another interview with the *Daily Star*, it became obvious that it was all getting to be a bit much. 'I admit we might not be at Dermot's level right now, but he is the best there is, no one is better in my opinion,' she said. 'We've only had five weeks, Dermot had eight years. I knew stepping into Dermot's shoes would be impossible; I wouldn't say it's a poison chalice but I knew we'd be criticised. I never took the job thinking I was a better presenter than Dermot but I had to take the risk and rise to the challenge. People also need to remember Olly is a pop star, not a presenter, but he's doing brilliantly. We come off buzzing and it isn't until you then hear all the negative comments that you doubt yourself. Simon's really pleased with us. I find him really easy to work with.'

In December, Caroline was named ultimate TV personality of the year at *Cosmopolitan*'s Ultimate Women of the Year Awards, and spoke of the fact that women are under far more pressure than men when they appear on TV – she had yet again been trolled by people telling her she was fat.

When it came to the final of *X Factor*, there were technical glitches and Caroline was overheard asking for guidance. This prompted yet more criticism, while Simon appeared to be lifting his hands in despair. It was a dismal end to an unhappy experience. Louisa Johnson was finally crowned the victor, but it was clear something had to change.

And it did. There had been speculation that the show would be binned altogether after ratings for the final had been disappointing, but that was never going to happen. It was far too successful and what was needed was a rethink. And so, to no one's real surprise, it emerged that Caroline and Olly would not be presenting the show the following year. Instead … Dermot O'Leary was back for what would be the show's thirteenth series. 'I'm very flattered to be asked back to *The X Factor*, and am currently dusting off my dancing shoes,' he said in a statement. 'There is nothing more exciting than hosting live TV on a Saturday night. The show is naturally very close to my heart, after having hosted it for eight years. I'm really looking forward to it, and excited to be back.'

It might have been a disappointing episode for both Olly and Caroline, but she had other pans in the fire. And they were on an island that was hot, hot, hot …

10

LOVE ISLAND

Way back in the mists of time – or 2005, to be exact, ITV had an idea: send twelve single celebrities to spend five weeks on an island in Fiji and see how they all got on. Proposed as a rival to the then wildly successful Big Brother, the first series of *Celebrity Love Island* attracted controversy from the start: the celebrities weren't that famous, it was said, they were also not the most riveting of people, they were treating the trip as a free holiday and the presenters, Kelly Brook and Patrick Kielty, were said not to get on.

Worse still, ITV moved *Coronation Street* from its 7.30 p.m. slot to 8.30 p.m. to work as a lead-in to the show – prompting outrage – ratings were bad and, to cap it all, the live eviction show had to be cancelled when a storm blew up and six-foot waves prevented the crew from reaching the islanders. Jayne Middlemiss and reality TV personality Fran Cosgrave won but the series was not deemed to be a conspicuous success.

Nonetheless, a second series was commissioned the following year with a few tweaks. The length of the show was increased from five to seven weeks, Fearne Cotton was brought in to present with Kielty, Jayne Middlemiss hosted

Aftersun on ITV2 and 'celebrity' was dropped from the title, having been something of a hostage to fortune. Various ploys were used to increase the ratings, including bringing back former contestant, actor Paul Danan, who had been involved with Lady Isabella Hervey in the first series (confusingly, her sister Lady Victoria was in the new series). They also brought back contestant Calum Best, who started a romance with fellow contestant Bianca Gascoigne (fittingly, both were the offspring of famous footballers), brought the evicted Lady Victoria back to confront another contestant, model Sophie Anderton, over 'moving in' on her man and adding *Jackass* star Steve-O to the bunch. Steve walked out after two days after not being allowed enough chocolate and alcohol. The winners were Bianca and Callum and the runners-up were Kéllé Bryan and dancer Brendan Cole. Even second time around, the show didn't get very good reviews, was compared negatively to *I'm A Celebrity* and its ratings were only about half those of *Big Brother*. The show was at last cancelled. And that, conventional wisdom would have it, was that.

Except … it wasn't.

Fast-forward the best part of a decade and in February 2015 it was announced that *Love Island* would return, this time to ITV2, with more tweaks. In the new format the contestants would not even claim to be celebrities. This time around, members of the public would take part in a program narrated by comedian Iain Stirling. A couple of months later it was announced that Caroline, still riding high on the success of *Strictly*, would be the host. 'I can't wait to host the revamped *Love Island*,' said Caroline. 'I was a massive fan of the original show, and I'm sure this is going to be one crazy, love-fuelled island. I can't really think of a better way to spend a summer – here's hoping it's a scorcher!'

The format was as follows: a group of contestants, known as islanders, were put in a villa in Mallorca, cut off from the rest of the world. Located in Sant Llorenç des Cardassar, the islanders were under constant surveillance from sixty-nine cameras in a villa containing a bedroom and beds outside, a 'hideaway' bedroom where couples could spend the night as a reward, an interview room called the 'beach hut' where islanders could talk to the outside world and the 'pod' inside the villa where islanders could get messages from home. In order for the islanders to survive in the villa, they had to couple up with each other with a view to winning £50,000, They were called upon to be pragmatic as well as romantic as part of the show.

Contestants were introduced on the first day and coupled up. Over the course of the competition they were forced to 're-couple' – they could choose to stay with their original partner or make a change. Any unfortunate singleton left after the coupling was booted out of the villa and were also voted out by viewers. In the first of the new series, Caroline hosted a weekly live episode, in which some contestants were dismissed and new ones brought in (this was dropped in subsequent seasons). Meanwhile, each islander had their own phone from which they could text the others to receive news on re-couplings and all also had to take part in a series of games and challenges. Occasionally, they were allowed outside the villa on a date.

Caroline was asked why the celebrity element had been taken out. 'It's more relatable for people when they watch,' she explained to *Metro*. 'I want viewers to feel how the people in the show are feeling. That "I really like him but he likes the other girl" thing.' Would there be canoodling? 'Quite possibly, yes. But it's not going to be car-crash viewing because loads of shocking things are going on. We want it to show proper feelings.' In the event, there was footage that was too steamy to be shown, almost inevitable given the nature of the show.

The new show kicked off on 7 June 2015 with a live episode that saw the islanders entering the villa and it was immediately clear that, while they might not actually be celebrities as such, they most certainly had the looks. Some were models, all were buff, toned, manicured and immaculately styled: one thing the men and women had in common was that they were spectacularly attractive, sometimes quite unrealistically so. Indeed, the show was to provoke criticism that it was promoting false expectations of what a body could look like, but that did not impede its success. Indeed, it was an immediate hit with the viewers and in the years since its debut has turned in to ITV2's biggest show.

And in the middle of it all was Caroline, lively and engaging and cheerfully asking the islanders if they were ready for love. In retrospect, it was ironic. Caroline was being put through the mill herself on the subject of romance and she had been very publicly hurt over negative comments about her own body. Yet here she was, surrounded by gorgeous young men and women, all in a quest to find love. Or at least, to win £50,000 – love would be a bonus.

So, step forward Caroline the matchmaker. How would she do? 'I have match-made before, a couple of times,' Caroline told the *Daily Express*. 'Sometimes I get it really wrong. I remember dating a guy once and thinking, He's not my type, and thought, But my friend would like him. So I let her go on a date with him afterwards. She was so insulted, though, after she'd been on the date with him. I don't like anything too set-up, as that can get a bit awkward. I went to a hotel with my boyfriend at the time and, as a surprise, the hotel gave us our own table in the middle of the bandstand, surrounded by violinists and rose petals. Everyone else was eating off the bandstand – it was the most awkward experience.'

The new version of *Love Island* was determined to be a success and industry figures were talking it up, insisting it would not make for downmarket TV. ITV boss Angela Jain was keen to stress that the show was about relationships, not sex. How raunchy would it get? 'It depends on them – but it's not about that,' she said. 'What we are looking for is romance. I don't really want to show that kind of stuff. It is not the act that is interesting it's the reaction. That's the story. It's on at 9 p.m., not 11 p.m. Showing people shagging is pretty boring. I don't think that's an interesting way of telling a story. There are obviously compliance rules but, over and beyond that, it's whether it's right to show it and I don't want to show that, there is no joy in that and I want to show joyful stories.'

And so the contestants paraded to the villa. The girls were made up of community sports officer Lauren Richardson (she had been linked One Direction's Zayn Malik), marketing executive Danielle Pyne, former athlete Rachel Christie (niece of Linford) and models Zoe Basia Brown, Hannah Elizabeth and Jessica Hayes. The boys were groundsman Jordan Ring, joiner Joshua Ritchie, (his celebrity crush was Caroline), model and club promoter Chris Williamson, IT recruiter Omar Sultani, builder Jon Clarke and events company owner Luis Morrison.

The concept was not without cruelty, in that in pitting the contestants against each other for love, it addressed issues of physical attraction and set challenges designed to split established couples. Lauren, for example, was seen in tears when no one chose her. The link with Zayn had worked against her – the two had been pictured in Thailand a few months previously, although she was adamant nothing had actually happened. But the pictures provoked a furore, with Lauren even being blamed for Zayn's decision to leave One Direction. As she herself put it, the reaction was 'absolutely mental'.

Meanwhile, as all the islanders assembled, there was still some fascination about Caroline's own love life, which was going through a low. And while she was able to make a joke of it, there were clear signs that she wasn't that delighted with the state of affairs. 'Do you think they'll take advice from me?' she asked *Now* magazine. 'Girls, what you should do is wait until your mid-thirties and then find someone! And then get a cat.' And would she be taken with any contestant herself? 'I don't think so, strictly professional! I'm there for a shoulder to cry on – that's as far down as they can go! I'm not really into muscly men.' But would she be open to meeting anyone else while she was over there? 'Maybe. I don't know. I might head to Magaluf and see what's going on.'

Of course, Caroline had been very open with the problems she had had when people criticised her figure and now she was on one of the most body-conscious shows on the planet. 'I just wouldn't want to be in a bikini on telly! The worst feeling ever,' she said, explaining that she didn't like working out. 'I find it really hard. I don't really like dieting. I think about it once I'm on holiday and I'm like, "I should have gone to the gym!" I don't feel unhealthy. But I suppose I could be in better shape if I changed my lifestyle.'

There was also curiosity about whether Caroline would go on such a show herself as a contestant. After all, the first series had featured celebrities. 'I'll stick to hosting!' she told the *Radio Times*. 'I don't think I could let TV come into my actual life. I think I'll find love somewhere else – not on telly. Although I do see the irony of my love life being zero when I'm hosting a dating show. It's the loveliest feeling in the world being in love, but it's equally fulfilling feeling completely happy on your own.'

People were extremely curious about all aspects of her life and Caroline was happy to open up about some of her more bizarre habits. 'Sometimes I drink gravy from the jug,' she told *You* magazine. 'I just make up some Bisto and have it as a drink. The other day, I was too hungover to go out for a roast, so I went online and ordered dishes that had all the separate bits and when they arrived I removed each item – the meat from one dish, the potatoes from another – assembled them on a plate and whacked some gravy on top. I love really trashy takeaway food.' And her worst-ever job? 'Picking daffodils. I had to fill up a crate, which would take two hours, and I'd get fifty pence per crate. I lived in the country and that was the only job there was. But you do what you have to earn money. Having your own cash and responsibility is so important. I think I spent every penny of my wages in Tammy Girl. I've had all sorts of bad jobs since then. I've even been a magician's assistant.'

And what about new methods of finding a long-term love? In many ways *Love Island* harked back to an older way of doing things, as it involved matchmakers and people meeting each other in person. These days, of course, so much is done online. Would Caroline go online? 'My friend is on Tinder and I did loads of swipes so she has loads of people,' she said. 'But I have never done it. I think I am old-fashioned and I like to get into a conversation with someone and get to know them that way.'

But some healthier habits had begun to take hold. 'I'm off booze and have been for a few weeks,' she told the *Irish Sun*. 'I'm really enjoying it and have got so much to focus on that I plan to keep it up.'

Back on the show, the mind games soon began and the viewers tuned in. *Love Island* was gaining something of a cult following, especially among younger viewers. A few highlights to give a taste of the drama: some days into the contest, Italian identical twins John and Tony Alberti arrived; the islanders were told two men – those not in couples – would have to go. Elsewhere, islanders switched between one another with enthusiasm – Lauren was again in tears when Jordan, who had paired off first with Zoe, took up with her before going back to Zoe. Zoe confessed all to Lauren.

'I knew something was up, it was obvious,' replied Lauren. 'It puts me with nobody, if that makes sense. But if Jordan likes you and you like Jordan, there's no point me staying with Jordan. If it comes to it and you pick Jordan there's no point me going, "Oh, yeah, I want Jordan," because he ain't going to pick me, he's not going to be happy with me. But if you potentially see something there and he sees something in you then, yeah, go for it. I'm not going to be like, "You're a big bitch, I hate you." I ain't fighting over a guy.'

That was the sort of exchange that pulled in the punters and Lauren was also serenaded by a One Direction song, in a nod to her passing acquaintance with Zayn Malik. The tune came in the form of a parody of 'What Makes You Beautiful' (Caroline could have sympathised over being teased in that way). Lauren was also tasked with choosing which two men had to go.

'I just feel like today is D-day,' she said. 'I'm not being funny. I've been one of them that's been passed from pillar to post and I'm still in limbo. I just feel like all of them are going to pay me attention now because obviously I can save them. This is why I'm finding it so hard to say, "I'd really like to get to know him." I'm in the worst situation. They say I have the power. This power's a bad power to have.'

In the end the Italian twins went and played up to their role beautifully. 'We knew, going into the house, that we were going to end up being the bad guys, the game-players – that's what we wanted to do,' Tony told the *Evening Standard*. 'We wanted to go in there, cause havoc, you know. As soon as we got in there everyone was threatened by us, the guys were jealous of us, the girls didn't trust us at all. It's difficult to get into there and try and steal the girls off the guys.'

'Yeah, well, when we went in there we had a game plan, we knew what we wanted to do,' added John. 'We knew we were going to try and steal the guys' girls and on the dates we did exactly that. We were romancing the girls, charming them, sweeping them off their feet on the dates – it showed it works, the guys got pied [dumped] and we got the girls off them.'

All the contestants played the same game. Omar was desperate to stay in and so played up to both Lauren and Rachel: 'I don't want you to feel that I was talking to you yesterday because of this whole situation, because I've always spoken to you. I've always bantered you,' he said to Lauren, 'because I know Chris has only just started speaking to you yesterday, really, wasn't it, and the twins you've probably had chats with them, but I genuinely did speak to you anyway, irrespective of what's going on. I just don't want you to feel like I'm faking it or anything.'

Two new girls, Naomi Ball and Daisy Muller, were sent in: 'I've been single about a year,' said Naomi to the *Mirror*.

'My friends call me a bit of a dater. I have been known to go on five dates a week. I would give myself a nine out of ten for looks all dressed up but next morning all hungover, I'm struggling for a three. The boys I like are arrogant, cocky and good-looking. It makes me laugh when girls say that they only have guy mates because in my head I'm just thinking, "You're a slut." I definitely want to make a bang when I go into the villa, I want to shake things up. If I put my mind to something or someone I definitely get them.'

Daisy said, 'I've been single all my life, but now I think it's time for somebody else to pay the bill. I'm looking for a man that has ambition, he knows what he's doing. He's confident. Men should have charm. All my friends are guys. I think I'm quite laddish in a way. If I go into the villa and there's a guy that I like, he will definitely be mine at the end of the day.'

Viewers were fascinated and, while ratings were quite low by comparison with later series, the word about the show was beginning to get out. The contestants may not have been professional celebrities but they certainly knew how to make good television. Blistering rows always went down well – as demonstrated when Hannah found her boyfriend, Jon, lying with his head on Naomi's lap. 'I shouldn't have let Naomi play with my hair, that was strange that she did it,' explained Jon later. 'Of course, Hannah's gonna be fuming about that, it's not right. If she was sitting on someone's lap, I'd be fuming about it.'

Hannah was not appeased: 'You wanna sit round flirting with other people in front of my f**king face? Imagine I did that with, like, Omar? If you think it's going too fast, you're the one who asked me to be your bird. Stop making a tit out of me, telling me one thing one day which is quite heavy. If you wanna do that maybe you shouldn't have asked me to be your girlfriend. I just think if it was the other way round, you'd probably have a problem with it. It just shows that I wouldn't have the disrespect to do that!'

The producers showed themselves to be pretty ruthless, too. Daisy Muller and Chris Williamson were turfed out when they were single. Both lashed out at the show. 'I'm happy to be dumped,' said Daisy. 'The guys there are not the people I'd usually mix with anyway. They're immature. Jordan's a p***k and acts like a knob.'

Chris said the contestants were becoming 'telly tubbies': 'No-one's controlled their diet. You're in the sun all day enjoying yourself eating and drinking.'

A newbie, Cally Jane Beech, was introduced into the mix and various initiatives were introduced to keep the viewers riveted. Towards the end of June, Calum Best, who had been the winner of the original show a decade previously, turned up unexpectedly: '*Love Island* … What's up!' he cried.

Jess Hayes explained they were delighted at this surprise: 'We're in the villa, going about our own business, and who rocks up? Calum-f**king-Best.'

'So, I was lucky enough ten years ago to take part in the original *Love Island*, and I ended up winning it, so it was a great experience, great memories,' said Callum, before revealing the masterstroke intended to divide the boys and the girls. 'Boys … you and me are going for a night out in Magaluf. Let's go!'

The girls were not so delighted to be left out, fearing that the temptations placed in front of their beaus would be too much. 'Jon did give me a hug and a kiss, but not enough for my liking,' said Hannah, plaintively.

'He would never f**k you over,' said Zoe.

'Even though me and Max aren't that serious, I want him back here – right now,' said Jess. Zoe attempted to reassure her. Max, she said, 'won't mug her' because 'he's a really nice boy'. Yet the fretting went on.

Meanwhile, the islanders shared their innermost thoughts in the beach hut where Naomi, seeing the reaction of her fellow islanders as the boys took off for the bright lights, shared her relief she was not in their number, as she had split up with Josh. 'The girls just kind of lost the plot ... I'm actually so relieved that I'm not with Josh now because I would be sh**ting myself, a night out in Magaluf ... '

The fun continued: newlywed former *TOWIE – The Only Way is Essex –* star Mark Wright turned up at the villa to DJ at Lauren Richardson's birthday party, shortly before the show finished in early July. The producers had been reintroducing exes to the villa in an attempt to provoke yet further tension. Josh and Max were told they were to meet five dinner dates and one of them turned out to be Jasmine, Jordan's former girlfriend. He did not look thrilled: 'Seriously! It's like a ghost from the past has just strolled through the villa.'

A row (inevitably) ensued: 'All I wanted was closure, I didn't want to get back with you,' said Jasmine.

'I gave reasons, you weren't listening to my reasons ... we weren't working out, I couldn't see a future with you and it takes a stronger person to end it if it's going nowhere,' protested Jordan

'I knew I'd never get any apology for the way you treated me,' said an emotional Jasmine.

'I never treated you bad once in the relationship whatsoever,' protested Jordan.

'How can you sit here and say this Jordan?' cried Jasmine. 'No matter what you did to me I could never f***king hurt you, and all I was asking from you is just closure and you wouldn't talk to me, you dumped me by text.'

'I told you face-to-face!' protested Jordan

'Did you f***!' said Jasmine, somewhat gracelessly.

'You're getting angry now, I'm walking away,' said Jordan.

'You f***ing screwed me over you d***head,' yelled Jasmine. The viewers lapped it up.

As the series climaxed, the stakes were getting high. Jon and Hannah seemed to be loved-up – so much so that they were going to get engaged. 'For us to win *Love Island* as a couple would just finish off the fairytale story that we've started,' said Jon in a direct appeal to the viewers. 'We met each other the first day, we've come on in leaps and bounds, we've got to know each others' sh*t bits, ugly bits, bad bits, great bits, lovely bits, sexy bits … you've watched us grow as a couple into where we are now.'

'I've met the love of my life and winning *Love Island* would just help start our future together,' said Hannah.

The big moment unfolded on screen. 'Hannah, we have been together from day one and I fell in love with you straight away,' said Jon. 'You are my princess, my world, and I love you so much. I've written you a poem: "Love is mad, love is crazy, love makes me feel like a daisy. Love is scary, love is cool though, loving you makes me feel like a rainbow. Every day you give me the horn, and every day I feel like a unicorn. My love for you is from the heart, even though I always fart. My love for you will never end, 'til the day I meet my end." And, obviously, I've met you and you're the woman of my dreams. Hannah, would you do the honour of making me the happiest man alive and marry me?'

Hannah would.

'Of course I would. Oh my God. Oh my God. You're the best man I've ever met in my entire life. I f***ing love you to pieces. Yes, I'll be your wife,' she cried.

The series finished on 15 July 2015, although it was not the engaged couple but rather Jess Hayes and Max Morley who were the winners: they were both offered the chance to share or steal the prize money in a slightly complicated format that meant they risked losing it. Both wisely chose to share. Of the final couples, Cally Jane Beech and Luis Morrison were the first ones to leave, coming fourth (they became the first couple from the show to have a baby together, in 2017). Lauren and Josh came third and newly engaged Jon and Hannah were second.

Straight out of the villa, Jess and Max did not exactly sound as if they were on the verge of a brand-new future: 'We have a laugh together but we are not madly in love or anything like that,' Jess told Mirror Online, touching on the fact that they lived in different parts of the country. 'We are not going to move in together or anything like that – it's a bit soon. I've been in a long-distance relationship before and I think they can work out better sometimes. Anyway, I travel a lot with my job.'

All the couples subsequently split up.

11

LOVE ISLAND (PART TWO)

While no one pretended that contestants on *Love Island* were going to end up as fellows of All Souls College, Oxford, the programme had been a resounding success. It had attracted a fair bit of grumbling from the critics for not being perhaps the most highbrow show on television. Nor had ratings been stratospheric, but enough viewers, especially younger ones, loved it. The following year, however, it was to become a national obsession, one that Caroline was to be associated with until the end of her life.

However, it was to be months before she was to be summoned back to the island and there was still a living to be earned. Caroline remained, of course, heavily involved in *The X Factor*, but there were other matters keeping her busy. She took part in the 2015 Text Santa initiative, which had been set up by ITV to support UK charities; she was one of a number of presenters, including Phillip Schofield, Holly Willoughby and Olly Murs. She made guest appearances on *Ant & Dec's Saturday Night Takeaway* and in May she made a leap to radio when she began co-presenting *Sunday Morning Breakfast* from 9 a.m. to noon with Gethin Jones across the Heart network, standing in for Stephen Mulhern and Emma Willis as the latter took maternity leave. The deal was thought to be worth £100,000. 'Heart FM have been after Caroline for a while. They've offered her loads of money and reckon they've struck gold, pairing her with Gethin,' a source told the *Mirror*. 'Producers are hoping they will be the station's next hit duo. It's likely to be a temporary position to begin with, but station bosses are hoping she stays for the long haul.'

Everyone pitched in with the usual enthusiasm. 'Heart has a brilliant presenter line-up and I'm thrilled to be joining the team with Caroline,' said Gethin. 'It's great to be back on the radio and I know we're going to have a lot of fun with our listeners.'

Caroline said, 'Sunday mornings are the perfect time for listening to feelgood tunes and having fun, and I've always wanted to work in radio so I'm incredibly excited about our new show on Heart.'

Gary Stein, managing editor of Heart, said, 'Gethin and Caroline are two of the country's most popular presenters so I'm delighted they've chosen to join Heart. There's a brilliant chemistry between the two of them and I know their energy and charisma will bring a real feel good vibe to Sunday mornings on Heart.'

But behind the scenes not all was well. With increased success came increased pressure and when she alluded to the fact that she had quit alcohol during the filming of *Love Island*, Caroline was admitting she might be prone to overdoing it at times. Indeed, this proved to be the case, with Caroline have to go to a detox retreat in April 2016. 'I used to turn to wine if I had a stressful day,' Caroline told the *Sun*, admitting that the criticism she and Olly had taken over their presenting of *The X Factor* had taken its toll. 'I acted like it's a treat. But it's not a treat. You're covering up your stress rather than dealing with it. I wasn't looking after myself. I wasn't feeling a hundred per cent healthy or a hundred per cent happy.' The detox had worked well for her. 'I've had a bit of a life-changing eleven weeks. Changed a lot about my thoughts and my body. I couldn't turn to someone and say fix me – I had to do that myself. I'm off booze and have been for a few weeks.'

But for how long? Shortly afterwards she was seen at the wedding of Sam Teasdale, sister of Caroline's friend Lou, the One Direction hair stylist. By all accounts, Caroline enjoyed a party binge that lasted a few days. There were also reports that she had been tweeting her ex Jack and then deleting the tweets; her new year resolution in that quarter had clearly not lasted.

She was also on Twitter in ways that were possibly more damaging than drinking too much. She had been subjected to some appalling vitriol, not least during *Strictly*, and she was clearly still reeling from it, yet she stuck to her feed. 'You can think social media is real life but you have to remember it's not,' she told the *Daily Record* of her time on the dance show. 'Someone wouldn't come up to you in the street and say, "You're a big, fat, ugly s***." Yet they find it really easy to say online. I can have the worst day ever, but I'll post the happiest picture of myself. My life is like a sad film. I cried after the first live Sunday night. The reaction was overwhelming because I didn't think people would be talking about how I look, how I stand, how I walk or how I laugh. But I've been in this industry for twelve years and you get used to the criticism. I know how the game works. Not everyone is going to like you all the time, not everyone is going to think you're beautiful. But there is a difference between opinion and abuse. Opinion is fine but I need to stop giving negative people airtime because they love it. I put myself out there and can't moan. I have a really good job and a really good life. The good bits outweigh the bad by a mile. If I couldn't handle any more, I would get out of the media industry.'

But it was getting to her far more than she wanted to admit and one problem was that Caroline engaged and lashed back. If she really had been able to walk away and ignore it that would have been one thing, but she didn't. She let it get under her skin.

Meanwhile, Caroline was not going to return to *The X Factor*: it hadn't worked and everyone involved knew it. But neither did she want to appear to be critical of one of the biggest shows on British television and nor was it a good idea to fall foul of the people involved in making it. And, so, she was keen to emphasise the fact that the time on the show had been a good one: '*The X Factor* was one of my best experiences,' she said. 'I loved every minute. Mistakes happen all the time. It's part of telly. So when things go wrong, people are always going to go, "It's your fault!"

'Simon gave me a big cuddle and said, "It's not your fault."

'I haven't decided about doing it again yet but everyone knows you don't talk about *X Factor* until later in the year. But I do want to do new things. I auditioned for the musical *Chicago*, which I got, but the timings didn't work. I've also always wanted to do a documentary about being a twin, something more factual.'

Caroline was now in her late thirties, which can be a tricky age for a television presenter, especially one so associated with youth programming. But, as she herself often pointed out, her mainstream television career didn't really get going until she had begun her fourth decade and this was not a problem for now. 'I've never been affected by ageism and if anything, in my twenties I was always told that I looked too young,' she said. 'But everyone goes through dry spells and there may be a day when the phone stops ringing but, again, that's why we do this job. It's part of the excitement. In terms of female presenters, I have only ever experienced positivity – we are all really supportive of one another.'

Soon enough, *Love Island* loomed. In the lead up to the new run, Caroline's appearance had changed quite dramatically. Always conscious of the criticism of the trolls, and extremely body-aware, she had lost a stone and, while she had not been previously overweight, television did add pounds and she clearly wanted to prove the naysayers wrong. Along with the detox came personal training with Olympic athlete Sarah Lindsay. The difference in the way Caroline looked was huge. Indeed, the transformation was so great that it garnered coverage itself and Caroline was asked how she did it. Diet and exercise was the reply.

'I'm always starving in the morning, so I eat a lot for breakfast. It's usually scrambled or poached eggs, bacon, avocado, mushrooms or sometimes even steak,' she told *Your Fitness* magazine. 'Whenever I've worn bikinis in the past I've always thrown a vest over the top, especially if there's a lot of people around the pool. I'm consuming more calories now than ever before – they're just the right calories. What made the biggest difference to how I looked and felt was cutting out all sugar. I work out three times a week and used to feel really intimidated entering the free weights area but now I feel comfortable. I've been lifting heavy weights for fourteen weeks and I haven't become any bigger.

'The truth is I did this for me – to make myself feel the very best I could and this is the way I decided to do it.'

In fact, around mid-2016, Caroline appeared to be obsessed with two things: social media and her weight (and the two were linked.) She had been named as the face of the Speedo Sculpture swimsuit and did a number of interviews on the back of it, all of them hinting at an underlying insecurity that simply wouldn't go away. Not that she wasn't, as always, putting a very brave face on it.

'Well, if you didn't develop a thick skin in this job you would live in misery,' she told the *Mirror*. 'Part of my job is to be judged. I put myself out there. I try to not pay too much attention.' In response to jibes about overeating, she just wanted to say to the bullies, 'I've acknowledged what you have said, and I'm glad I would never be that horrible to others. I don't understand it. I feel awful if I think I have made someone feel bad. How you make others feel is the biggest reflection of who you are. There is nothing better than being nice. It's just so good for other people … I had an agent who said to me, "You've let yourself go a bit," and at the time I was happy and in a good place. That's probably why I'd let myself go. That annoyed me.'

It seemed that the new radio show was giving her the jolt she needed to get herself back in shape. 'I wasn't living a healthy lifestyle – I was indulgent, eating what I wanted, staying up till 4 a.m., getting up at midday. It was fun, but you can't live like that for ever,' she said. It was also not possible to sustain a high-pressure career living like that, something of which Caroline was clearly aware. She had implemented a regime that included not only a healthier diet but dance, free weights and yoga. 'I saw the nutrition plan and was like "*What*?!"' she continued. 'I didn't realise there was so much sugar in everything. I used to walk into the gym, look at a machine and be too embarrassed to try it. Now I'm in the weights area with the men using dumbells. If an alien was looking down at our magazines he'd think we have just one body shape. But women come in different sizes and shapes. I'll always have a bit of a belly and I'll always have that fear when I walk away from someone – "Don't look at my bum."'

There spoke the girl next door.

Summer 2016 was taken up with the second series of *Love Island*, which ran from 30 May to 11 July and ran every night of the week, with the Saturday episode used as a weekly catch-up called *Love Island: The Weekly Hot List*. The word was truly out about this new sensation now, and ratings averaged just under 1.5 million viewers, up 900,000 from the last time round.

The eleven contestants lined up to go in, all the twenty-somethings looking for love. They were Miss Great Britain Zara Holland, Scott Thomas, a twenty-seven-year old entrepreneur, thirty-year old Sophie Gradon, who had had a brief relationship with Danny Cipriani (of whom more anon) and who also was a previous Miss Great Britain, make-up artist Malin Andersson, circus performer Cara De La Hoyde (who also worked on adult TV) and sales executive Olivia Buckland. Boys included carpenter Nathan Massey, osteopath-turned-model Daniel Lukakis, barman and fitness instructor Tom Powell, surveyor Javi Shephard, and Rykard Jenkins, a personal trainer from Kent.

Highlights (or low lights, depending on your point of view) included the first time an islander was removed from the villa (Malia Arkian, after a row with Kady McDermott), as well as voluntary departures: Rykard Jenkins left after his love interest, Rachel Fenton, departed and Zara Holland had to go due to a family illness. Sophie Gradon went after a row with Katie Salmon: the pair had been the programme's first same-sex couple but split after a row over a man (Sophie also had a boyfriend).

As usual they all had ideas of what they were looking for: 'I've never been in love,' said Javi. 'I feel like I'm so passionate, I would give everything to the right girl. And I've just never felt like that. She has to be perfect! She has to be intelligent, athletic and healthy, and just have something about her. She should just be fun. I want a girl with good energy, who makes me happy.'

Rykard knew who he didn't want: 'Girls who are self-obsessed, who care too much about their image, and take themselves too seriously. That's just boring to be around. If they've got nothing to offer other than how they look, then I lose interest.'

And Caroline was as enthusiastic as ever about her charges: 'Everything moves so fast in there,' she said. 'Relationships are so interesting when you get to see everything and you get to see them develop and change right from the start.' But she didn't like it when it got too intimate. 'I had to have my fingers in my ears for certain parts. I could watch it no problem, but I preferred watching it to listening to it. I don't like hearing those noises!'

The housemates soon kicked off. Malin, to the viewers' astonishment, was the last woman to be picked. Scott, meanwhile, zoomed in on Zara: 'I'm going to throw this out there now and I mean this genuinely but I want to be the first person to kiss on *Love Island*,' he said. 'Do you mind if I kiss you?'

Zara did not and, to cheers from the other islanders, they had a snog.

Secrets tumbled out. Sophie had paired off with Tom, but revealed that she had in the past dated women. Zara and Tom got together but it didn't last: 'I'm going to have to be honest with you now,' he explained in one of those cringe-making exchanges the show was becoming famous for. 'On paper, you're amazing. But I think me and you are missing something. You're absolutely mint but I've got to be completely honest with you. I'm not a touchy-feely guy and I think you need somebody loving. Do you understand? I feel like I'm being fake. You deserve better. You're selling yourself short.'

A tattooed newbie appeared in the form of a lad named Terry Walsh, who caught Olivia's eye. Another late arrival was Kady McDermott: 'I say it how is it and I'm straight to the point,' she said. 'I'm a bit like Marmite because not everyone likes that.'

The obligatory rows entertained the audience. On a 'date', Scott and Kady had a tiff for the cameras that revealed some surprisingly traditional views on Scott's part: 'I think you're a bit of a serial dater,' he said. 'You can spend time with different guys quite easily and you're quite comfortable with that.'

'Wow, you think I'm a proper game-player, don't you?' Kady replied.

Scott told Kady their situation was 'temporary': 'You know what I wish now? I wish I'd stayed with Zara and I would have seen your f***ing true colours.'

'Zara would go back with you in a heartbeat, so f*** off,' Kara replied.

'Yesterday I really fancied you,' said Scott, continuing less than gallantly, 'I don't know why, must be cabin fever but I thought you were fit.' Later, in the beach hut, he said,

'I'm cringing about the fact that I'm laying in bed with her, kissing her and then in a couple of weeks she might be laying there with someone else kissing them. And I don't like that. Right now, I've not got it under control. At some point I will though.'

Kady also spoke in the beach hut: 'I was sitting at dinner and instead of thinking I'd love to kiss you, I was thinking, I'd love to punch you right in the face, you annoying b*****d.' The course of true love never runs smooth.

Javi was the first to be evicted after Zara chose Dan: 'I want to couple up with this boy because I want to get to know him more,' said Zara. 'I have to go with my heart and my head on this one. The boy I want to couple up with is . . I'm really sorry, I hate letting people down, but I have got to go with Dan.' Javi wept.

Malia, a late arrival, was sent packing after a row with Kady over spilled wine. She had spent less than a day on the show. And the games continued: Terry was coupled with Olivia but had spent time chatting to Malin: what, inquired Olivia, had they been talking about?

'Just getting to know her,' said Terry cautiously. 'I've not had the chance to properly get to know anyone. It was nice to get to know her. It was good. We've got a lot in common. It's just easy, there's no shying away from that fact. It's early doors right now. We've only got things going for the last forty-eight hours. I don't know how you're feeling. I don't know you really. I'm comfortable with you and have a good time with you, but I don't know you. You know who I'd have gone with, obviously. Malin. When I came in from the start I said it was you or Malin.' He repaired to the beach hut. 'I said from the start, me and Olivia have a lot in common and I've got along with her and I feel comfortable with her, but in the next breath I want to see Malin,' he pondered. 'It feels a bit more deeper when I'm with Malin than it is with Olivia. I feel like Olivia could be my best mate and Malin could be my girlfriend. I always gauge it on butterflies, and I never really got massive butterflies with Olivia. I do enjoy her company, and that's why I'm cut up about hurting her because I don't really wanna do that. But I don't really know what other road to take right now.'

The intrigue sent the viewing figures shooting up. Rykard had been heartbroken over Malin but was making a quick recovery courtesy of Olivia. But Rachel, coupled with Dan, was interested in Rykard too. 'Obviously, I fancied Dan before I came in here but meeting him on that date, it was more kind of like a friend … he's quite a friendly person. So I don't know,' she told Malin. She continued in the beach hut: 'Obviously, Daniel I was initially really attracted to him and I still am, I think he's gorgeous, but Rykard I think he's been the person that surprised me the most, how I wasn't initially attracted to him and then when I've seen him and he's been quite friendly, he's actually quite sweet and endearing in a way. I'm definitely attracted to Rykard. I really didn't think I would be but he is kind of my type. Dark hair, dark eyes. That's what I usually do go for in a guy and, yeah, I do find him attractive, definitely. He's got amazing teeth. When you get to know someone's personality, and when you get to know them a bit better, they become even more attractive to you. I think that's what probably could happen. He's just really sweet.'

Elsewhere, Rykard was sharing: 'When she [Rachel] come in I thought she was like the elf out of *Lord Of The Rings*. That beautiful blonde long hair, posh and she spoke so nicely and do you know what … proper lady.'

'Rachel's a very attractive girl,' said a thoughtful Tom. 'I think Rykard's had a cheeky little look. He's kind of single. He's with Liv but they're not finding that attraction to each other, they're still in the friend zone, both of them. So I think he is kind of looking for a girl.'

'I believe that you'll make me have fun,' Rachel told Rykard.

'I'll make you happy, don't worry about that,' replied Rykard. 'You've made such an impression. You woke up this morning and you looked like an angel. All your blonde hair.'

In the beach hut, Rykard said: 'I think Rachel's fit, one hundred per cent. Look at her, she's gorgeous, man. She's beautiful. Tall, smart, long blonde hair, do you know what I mean? Banging body.'

Of course, Rykard was actually technically still with Olivia: 'It's just another thing that I'm caught up in that I don't want to be caught up in,' Olivia told Sophie.

Olivia moved to the beach hut: 'I don't know if Rachel likes Rykard or not. I think she would say that she does. Because the other couples are quite strong she sees a hole with me and Rykard. I just feel like such a gooseberry. I feel like the ugly apple. When there's a box of apples, I feel like the bruised apple and I'm just never being chosen.'

In the event Rachel was voted off and the usual emotional confrontations kicked off. As the weeks wore on, tempers were beginning to fray: there were even arguments about a cheese toastie and squabbles about what to wear. More new islanders arrived, including Alex Bowan, who made it very clear he was up for flirting with anyone. Indeed, more than flirting. There had been some disquiet about the fact that some of the islanders had been having sex on TV and within a very short time Alex and Zara counted themselves among them.

This caused a particular row, not just because the act was screened but due to Zara being Miss Great Britain. This was not how beauty queens were supposed to behave. Ultimately, she was stripped of the title, not that that did much to discourage the others. 'Zara is a lovely girl, we understand that this is out of character for her and that she truly regrets her actions; however, the decision simply comes down to the fact that she has broken the rules of the competition,' the beauty contest's executives said in a statement. 'Miss Great Britain works with charities, children and young, impressionable people; our title-holder must be an ambassador and this public behaviour does not support the ethos of our brand.' Zara was in tears when she relayed the news to the others in the villa; there was sympathy all round.

All this time, Caroline was commuting between England and Mallorca; her own life and appearance continued to attract as much speculation as before. Her show was by now the 'guilty secret' of many and a firm favourite – with one columnist asking on its conclusion, 'How will we live without it?' The winners that year were Cara De La Hoyde and Nathan Massey, who went on to feature in *TOWIE*, while Lex Bowen and Olivia Buckland were the runners-up. The following year Rykard joined the cast of *Ibiza Weekender*. It was a good result for all concerned and given the massive jump in ratings, the next series was immediately recommissioned. At the same time, Caroline was stepping into a brand new project – fulfilling an ambition she had held all her life.

12

GIVE 'EM THE OLD RAZZLE DAZZLE

It was in September 2017 that Caroline finally achieved her lifetime ambition of appearing in a musical, when she opened in a touring production of *Crazy For You* with the cast of the Watermill Theatre.

There had been rumours that some such production was in the pipeline: earlier in the year Caroline had been seen at the What's On Stage Awards with Paul Taylor-Mills, who was the artistic director of the Other Palace theatre, Victoria, and worked closely with Andrew Lloyd Webber. It was thought that, after all this time, she was finally determined to make a career on the stage. And she was. But she wanted to take it gradually and to learn her trade

When the moment finally came, Caroline very wisely chose a lighthearted, feel-good production and she went for a fairly small role at that. *Crazy For You* was a romantic comedy musical from the early 1990s that took the songs of George and Ira Gershwin with a book by Ken Ludwig and had won a slew of awards. Famous numbers included 'I Got Rhythm' and 'Nice Work If You Can Get It'. The show told the story of Bobby, the son of a rich banking family in New

York, who works in the bank but really wants to be a dancer on Broadway. Somewhat inexplicably, given this ambition, he is sent to the small town of Deadrock, Nevada to close a theatre down. However, he falls for the proprietor's daughter and decides to try to keep the theatre open by putting on a show. Caroline played Irene, the fiancée he jilts, who follows him across the country to try to get him back.

Her fitness regime was preparing her for this physical stage work as much as it had prepped her for *Love Island* and the radio show. This was her moment and she was determined to take it and also determined to put the partying lifestyle behind her. 'Work is all-consuming,' she told *You* magazine. 'I'm training to keep my fitness levels up, eating properly for the first time and working with a vocal coach and acting coaches so my voice and my performance will be as good as possible. I'm exhausted. If I do go out, I'll be more likely to see a play than party. I know this isn't something anyone would expect of me – people have only seen me presenting TV shows – but musical theatre is what I always wanted to do. And I want to show that I can do it well.' Indeed, she revealed that this had been a dream since early childhood. 'When I was a kid I sometimes performed at the local village hall, and we also used to go and see shows in Norwich and in the West End,' Caroline told *What's On Shropshire*, part of a publicity campaign that was to see her talking to the press all over the country. 'When I was about ten, I can remember asking my mum if people really did that as a job, and deciding that was what I wanted to do. So it's been in me since a really young age. I was really driven – I enrolled in loads of different classes and got myself a scholarship, but then when I left college I got snapped up by a TV agent.'

It had taken a long time to get on the stage and there was no doubt in Caroline's mind exactly how this had come about. '*Strictly* had a lot to do with where I am right now,' she told the *Sunday Post* of Scotland and the north of England. 'I was offered a few lead roles in productions, but I didn't feel ready to take on such big parts. I felt it was important to earn my stripes and gain experience, so when the role of Irene came along it felt perfect. It's not a big role – I'm probably on stage for the least amount of time out of everyone. It's Charlotte [Wakefield] who is the star.' She was to speak elsewhere about adopting the same approach in her television career: to take on smaller roles, leading up to the bigger ones. It was possible that she underlined this because the criticism she had received for taking on really big role, presenting *The X Factor*, still rankled.

Holby City star and fellow *Strictly* winner Tom Chambers played Bobby and Charlotte played Polly. And were there any similarities between her character, Irene, and Caroline herself? 'Irene is driven, and I suppose I am,' she muses. 'She knows what she wants, she's hurt the whole way through, and she's vulnerable but icy. I don't think I'm much like her but I can empathise. I don't think I would ever go across the country chasing after a man, though.'

She was certainly thrilled about the new development. 'Caroline's really keen to earn her stripes in theatre and has been seeing lots of different productions recently, including *Yerma* and *The Libertine*,' a source told the *Sun*. 'Next year is going to see a real shift for her. She's not moving away from television, but mixing telly with theatre. It's a dream she's been working on since she was a teenager and she's taking it very seriously.'

Caroline was happy to return to the comparison between her and Irene. 'She's strong. She knows what she wants. But there's a vulnerability,' Caroline told the theatrical expert and blogger Carl Woodward. 'She gets hurt the whole way through, but she's brilliantly defiant. She stays strong and doesn't give up. She's naughty as well. There's definitely bits of Irene that are quite like me.' And it was a perfect family show. 'It's feelgood and fun. It's a show the whole family can enjoy, but it's got a very cool vibe to it too. It's one of those shows where you will have a smile on your face the whole way through. I know, because I've seen the rehearsals. I think audiences will be blown away by the talent of the cast.' And she was looking forward to touring. 'I'm a traveller at heart. There is so much more to the UK than London and I don't get to see it enough, so I'm massively excited. There's some really amazing venues around the UK, and to play them will be hugely exciting.'

Choreographer Nathan M. Wright had created a routine for her, as well. It 'plays to her strengths. It's saucy and suggestive, but not too naughty'.

The tour set off in September and the reviews were positive, although critics were slightly taken aback not to see more of Caroline on stage. 'Tom Chambers is every inch the leading man,' wrote Andy Smart in the *Nottingham Post*. 'He oozes charm and charisma, dances with style and panache, and has a comedic ability bordering on the brilliant, at one point drawing on the legacy of Buster Keaton for a few extra laughs. Caroline Flack, surprisingly, has much less to do, with only one song, the cheeky "Naughty Baby", and few chances to show off some of her *Strictly* champion moves, but she still puts in an impressive turn.'

But her stage career was cut short, at least for a while. Just a couple of months into the tour, well before the production reached London, Caroline was forced to pull out due to ill health. 'I've had a wonderful time working on my first theatre tour,' she said in a statement. 'I've learned so much and can't wait for my next challenge on the stage. Unfortunately, I've had a rather nasty, recurring back injury and, with just five weeks remaining of my time with the show, I must reluctantly listen to doctor's orders. Thankfully, I'll be fighting fit again after a few weeks' rest. I feel very lucky it's not too serious.'

In the event, it was to be nearly a year before she took to the stage again, playing the vampish Roxie Hart in a revival of *Chicago* at the Phoenix theatre, taking over the role from Alexandra Burke until the end of its run. *Chicago* is one of the most successful musicals of all times, both recording the second-longest ever run on Broadway (after *The Phantom of the Opera*) and being the longest-running American musical in West End history. The show is set in the 1920s and tells the story of Roxie Hart and Velma Kelly, two murderous adventuresses who become celebrities of the vaudeville stage. It has won innumerable Tonys, among many other awards, and has also featured many of the great and good of Broadway and the West End in its cast over the many years it has run.

Roxie was a big part, played in the 2002 film by Renée Zellweger, and it was a major breakthrough for Caroline. She was thrilled: 'I've been imagining playing Roxie since I was a teenager,' she said. 'To have now landed the role in the West End is a dream come true. I hope I do everyone proud and don't fall off the ladder!' She only had an extremely limited time to learn the role: would she really be able to pull it off?

Yes. With a blonde wig and a black lace dress, she hoofed it with the best of them: 'I've just had one rehearsal with the band. The only rehearsal I get. I've had eight days to learn the show, one dress run and I go on tonight,' she posted on Instagram. In the event she carried it off, sharing pictures of flowers and her pet dog Ruby, who was sporting a sign around her neck. 'Hey Roxie Mommie. I wish you a great show tonight. I love you,' it read.

Caroline got great reviews from the public. Fans were struck not only by her dancing but by her powerful singing voice – the first time most people had heard it. She also got a big thumbs up from her co-star Todrick Hall, who was making his West End debut in the role of the lawyer, Billy Flynn. 'She's so awesome, so sweet so humble so down-to-earth and I think everybody in life, if they could take a little bite out of the Caroline Flack book it would be really helpful because she approaches everything with such an optimistic approach,' he told the *Mirror* in an exceptionally generous tribute. 'Like, she has learned the show faster than I think it has ever been done. Learning a lead character in eight days with such a specific type of vocabulary with choreography, it's just overwhelming for me to think about doing it and I've been doing theatre my whole life, so for someone who's never even done a musical before, is not a known singer, and your nerves get the better of you, and she has just come in here and done it like a pro and been so great to work with off stage. And she was the most calm I've ever seen anybody on opening night and for her not to be a musical-theatre-trained person is just remarkable.'

It was the culmination of a lifetime's dream and around the same time, fittingly, she featured in the *Strictly Come Dancing* Christmas special, this time performing with Gorka

Marquez (in the *Cinderella*-themed show, Ann Widdecombe and Anton Du Beke were the Ugly Sisters.) She easily coped with the change of partner but, as she was now hoofing it in musicals, returning to the TV show's style was quite a challenge. 'I was dancing with Pasha, but obviously he went quite far in the competition, so I'm with Gorka the corker,' she told Mailonline. 'My flexibility's gone a bit ... I found the ballroom the hardest, when you dance in hold you have to be in time with someone, but when do things like the charleston you're kind of on your own.'

But in the background, something far more worrying was going on. Caroline had been sufficiently open about her life and problems in the past for it to have been no secret that she suffered from depression – and at that time it was serious. To make matters worse, and in an echo of what happened in her love life at the time she won *Strictly*, her debut in *Chicago* came just as she finally split from her on-off boyfriend Andrew Brady, of which more in the next chapter, another relationship which caused her great angst. She revealed that she'd been so nervous taking on the role of Roxie that she'd had hypnotherapy to deal with her anxiety. She gave an emotional interview to the *Sun* that revealed quite how bad her depression had been and that she had been forced to use antidepressants in a bid to shake it off. She was brave to go so public with it, because it was still a condition that attracted a certain amount of stigma, but Caroline was clearly determined to have her say, much as she had when she discussed the difficult feelings with *Red* magazine.

'It all started the day after I won *Strictly*,' she told the *Sun*. 'I woke up and felt like somebody had covered my body in clingfilm ... Antidepressants helped me get up in the morning, and stopped me from being sad, but what they also do is stop you from being happy. So I was just in this numb state. I stopped laughing at jokes, and that's just not me. I came off them after six months, as I realised feeling something was better than feeling nothing at all.'

She had been taking anti-depressants again after having a panic attack in France. But she didn't tell anyone. 'I didn't want to be a burden,' she said. 'It was a really lonely place. While antidepressants can work for some people, I became a little too reliant on them – if you forget to take one, you feel awful. The only way I can describe it is that it was like going around a roundabout about three hundred times. They're a whirlwind for your body. I remember being at the photoshoot for my book cover and having to sit down because I was so dizzy. I couldn't tell anyone the reason, that I was coming off antidepressants. I eventually went to a juice retreat in the Mediterranean to wean myself off them. It was the only way I could get them out of my body.' It was a very far cry from the glossy Caroline everyone had been used to seeing – the inner turmoil she had been suffering was now on display for all to see.

She had also been extremely hurt by a joke Graham Norton had made at the 2016 Baftas about how unlikely it was that she would make a return to *The X Factor*. It was a rare example of Caroline not taking a joke well at all. 'I was sitting there in my dress, I didn't have a plus-one, and Graham's first joke was basically, 'There's more chance of Anne Boleyn returning to *Wolf Hall*,' she said rather stolidly. 'I'm sure it was quite funny but not so much when you're the person living that life, sat in the Baftas and the cameras are on you. I remember the person next to me touching my arm in sympathy, and just trying not to cry. I went home pretty much straight after. It was really horrible and my lowest point.'

But she was fighting the depression, which was not only in itself a dreadful problem for millions but came with other issues, particularly for someone seen so regularly in public. 'You would tell people if you have taken Nurofen or Lemsip, but not antidepressants,' she said. 'There's a stigma around it. I used to go to the chemist to collect my prescription on a Sunday, thinking the pharmacist had probably seen me on telly the night before. I was mortified, which I now know is ridiculous and was all in my head. I have a great life, a lovely house, and I know I am very lucky. I don't want anyone to ever think I am a victim, because I'm not.'

She was determined to prove it, too. Over Christmas 2018, she shared a picture of herself at church in Stoke Newington with her friends, the former One Direction hair-stylist Lou Teasdale and two male chums; they then spent Christmas Day serving lunch to locals. She posted: 'CHRISTMAS IN THE COMMUNITY … Spent the morning helping at this lovely church in Stoke Newington … @christmasmurdoch what a lovely day you have arranged.'

Her very well-received run in *Chicago* was coming to an end and Caroline made plans to head off to Thailand for a much-needed break in the sun. There was more instagramming, with Caroline sharing a picture of herself when she was fifteen with her father, 'When I was 15,' she wrote. 'Love you dada flack.' Thankfully, this did not encourage trolling: rather she was congratulated on how kind the years had been. By now she had 1.8 million followers as social media continued to play an enormous role in her life.

Caroline also put out another message in the wake of that Christmas Day, a somewhat wistful reflection of a year that had seen great highs but also great lows. She had been Roxie Hart, no less, in *Chicago*, but there had been a very painful end to a turbulent relationship. It was time to take it all on board and plan for the year ahead. 'It's been a crazy old year … I've had some of the best moments of my life in 2018 … and I won't forget it in a heartbeat … But as we get nearer to the new year it's a time for reflection and change … so gonna take me some time off after Chicago … Have a lovely Christmas and a happy new year … and remember to Choose Love.'

13

MEN, MEN, MEN

Caroline had attracted a fair bit of attention over her boyfriends. Prince Harry and Harry Styles had both excited comment for all the wrong reasons, and the relationship with Jack Street had not ended happily. But in October 2016, it emerged that there was a new man on the scene: Blue Logan.

Blue was an artist and illustrator who specialised in fashion and portraiture. His work had featured in magazines such as *Vogue* and *Elle*; he had had solo shows in London, New York and Los Angeles and his clients included Mastercard and Absolut Vodka.

It was Caroline who went public with the romance, posting a picture of the two of them with the caption 'You'll do, @ blue.logan' and more pictures of the two of them appeared, in Los Angeles and London, sometimes holding up one of Blue's illustrations. Another picture was captioned, 'Proud of this one … yes.'

'Caroline is so happy with Blue,' a source told the *Sun*. 'They've been enjoying each other's company and she's very proud of his work as an illustrator, not to mention how handsome she finds him. Blue has completely won over her friends. They all approve.'

But about three months into the relationship, the two drifted apart. Blue faded from Caroline's social media feed; she was instead featuring pictures of herself and a group of girlfriends on holiday in Thailand. 'Caroline and Blue have decided to split,' said a source. 'It was a mutual decision and there are no hard feelings. Both parties are happy and remain close friends.' It was back on the road again.

So it was that Caroline had been single for a while when, in early 2018, she switched on *Celebrity Big Brother*. A contestant caught her eye: reality TV personality Andrew Brady, and Caroline texted a friend to ask who he was. She then followed him on Instagram, and was followed back, with the line, 'Thanks for the support.' Another turbulent relationship was about to begin.

Andrew Brady had achieved a minor degree of celebrity when he appeared on *The Apprentice* in 2017. An aerospace engineer from Cheshire, he was eleven years Caroline's junior, but seemed to have an eye for older women – it had been rumoured that he had had a fling with fellow *Apprentice* contestant Anisa Topan, ten years his senior. The attraction between Caroline and Andrew was immediate and strong and they were inseparable. It was not to last.

To begin with, however, things were going very strong. Photographs began to appear on Caroline's social media, hinting that romance was in the air. They began to appear in public together. And, away from the public, matters were developing fast. 'People talk about meeting someone and feeling as though you've known them your whole life,' Caroline wrote in *Cosmopolitan*. 'That's what it felt like when I met you. I'll never forget seeing you walk into the restaurant

– tall, with a smile ten miles wide, not just for me but for everyone there. Talking to you was effortless. There were no first date nerves – just two people laughing and getting to know each other until the early hours. It was how all first dates should be.' The first date in question was to the cinema to see *The Shape of Water*.

As the romance gathered pace, Caroline was happy to be more public about it. She posted a picture of the two of them kissing in the snow. But theirs was a tumultuous affair. At first, the pair were extremely full-on; then there were rumours they had split in March over cheating, the episode taking place on social media. Caroline posted a heart emoji with the caption, 'Having tried to get rid of him for a while he's kinda just sticking around now'. This prompted a most unfortunate response: a woman claimed that Andrew had kissed her in a nightclub just two weeks previously. 'Ahh interesting,' she wrote. 'Got with him in rosies nightclub Chester when he did a appearance on Gay night, took me back to his. Then completely ignored me after. Lovely guy @CarolineFlack.' Caroline began following the woman on Instagram, who later said the two had been in touch. 'Yeah, we spoke, she wasn't angry with me at all.' She claimed that only kissing had gone on.

Caroline herself fuelled these rumours on social media: beside pictures of a forlorn-looking dog she posted the caption, 'Hey, pal. I know how you feel.' They were also pictured, clearly in the middle of a row. Whatever the truth behind the stories, it was plain that they hadn't been together that long before they had started having trouble.

Andrew point-blank denied everything, telling the *Sun* of the Chester story, 'I have never seen that woman in my life.' Meanwhile, the public weighed in on social media: 'If you go out with kids expect immature behaviour! Try a man, not a child!' 'You have to wonder why Flack keeps repeating behaviour that always has the same negative outcome. You'd think by now with her experience she could spot a determined, ambitious, Sleb Climber a mile away.' Another said, 'You need someone your own age Caroline!'

The trouble was that Caroline took these comments to heart. While she said in public that she ignored them, friends were later to reveal that she would spend hours poring over what people had said about her. There were also rumours that she was upset about the number of photographers who had begun to appear outside of her flat and she had begun wondering if they'd been tipped off.

Shortly afterwards, Andrew was pictured in the window of Caroline's flat; they were clearly back on. She followed him on Instagram again. In fact, they even seemed quite cheerful: they were photographed getting out of a taxi, looking all smiles; everything was racing ahead again. Some people remained concerned: was Andrew with Caroline for all the right reasons or did he want to boost his own profile?

The doubters upset Caroline so much she took to Twitter. 'I don't like to speak up on things. But. He's my boyfriend. And he's lovely to me. He's new to this world . No one is perfect. Give people a break … we all f**k up … all of us … people spend so much time over analysing things … let it be … you weirdos are taking time to write mean comments about someone you don't know … I'll get back to my love nest.'

In the middle of all this, it was announced that *Love Island* was soon to come back, while Caroline appeared with what seemed to be an 'AB' tattoo on her wrist. Events continued to move fast. After just three months together, Andrew proposed. A picture of the ring appeared on Instagram; 'He's put it on my finger and it won't come off. So I've said yes #chooselove.'

'Andrew proposed totally out of the blue and it was very low-key,' Caroline told the *Mail on Sunday*. 'I had no idea he was planning on asking me to marry him! But I knew things felt different in the lead-up; from the very first date with Andrew I felt as though I'd known him for years. I've never had that feeling before.'

As for that shot of him with his head out of the window: 'It wasn't a cry for help; his head was probably stuck out because I don't let him smoke indoors,' she protested. 'Look, the media go a bit crazy sometimes over nothing; this is my life. I've got one shot at it and I'm happy. That's all that matters. We all need to take the pressure off ourselves and become more accepting and less critical of other people's lives. I don't read people's opinion online because if you believe the good then you must believe the bad, so I choose not to believe any of it. I know what's in my heart. Let's enjoy life rather than bringing people down!'

Andrew's ex, Rachael Rhodes, certainly had something to say about all this. Andrew had been planning on proposing to her, she said, on top of which he had ghosted her after appearing on *Celebrity Big Brother* and then finished with her by text just two weeks before he met Caroline. 'How can you go from discussing marriage and babies with one woman to get engaged to another in just three months? Only Caroline will truly know how she feels about Andrew and what stuff he is saying to her but, if I was her, I'd be very concerned about the relationship and how true his intentions are,' she told the *Sun*. 'If the price of fame is a diamond ring, Andrew will happily pay that.'

Undaunted, Caroline and Andrew headed off to Santorini, Greece, for a holiday to celebrate their engagement, but shortly afterwards were seen in the middle of a blazing row. It blew over; next they were seen on a romantic boat ride. But speculation continued over the relationship: it emerged that Jack Street had become a father and friends of Caroline's wondered if she was rushing into a new relationship on the back of that. Caroline had said that she had 'big news' and people were even wondering if she was pregnant; instead it turned out she was signing a new business deal.

Another of Andrew's exes, Rachel Eglin, also spoke out. Behind the scenes there was trouble. 'I said, "Congratulations on the engagement,"' she told the *Mirror*. 'He was like, "It's not all it's made out to be. Things aren't great between me and Caroline. We always argue. But it's a great thing that's happened, meeting her." What he was saying was quite confusing. One minute he was saying it was s*** and not the life he wanted, and then he'd backtrack and say, "Caroline's the best person I've met in my life."'

In May, the *Love Island* machine cranked into action in earnest with the announcement of the line-up of initial contestants. Caroline landed in Majorca, amid a series of glamorous photoshoots. One of the contestants was Dani Dyer, daughter of actor Danny Dyer, with whom Caroline had appeared in *Is Harry on the Boat?* Caroline saw the funny side: 'The last time I met Danny Dyer I was in a film with him. If you google it you will see,' she told the *Sun*. 'I was only young. I was nineteen. I'm proud of everything I've done, but you may see a bit of nudity.' And she and Andrew might get married in the villa, she joked, as she was so hopeless at organising anything. Yet she was not actually going to be in

Majorca full time – the spin-off show *Aftersun* had begun and she was needed to present that.

The was the first time that Caroline presented *Love Island* while she was in a relationship herself and so her words took on added resonance as she said, 'Love is what we all eventually want; we relate to it, we look for it. In a way, *Love Island* has taken us back to the old-fashioned way of dating,' she told Mailonline. 'We all have a fascination with other people's relationships – even when we're at school, it's what we talk about.'

That was certainly true and the nation remained fascinated with Caroline's own love life, which was not always running smoothly. 'You'd maybe think I'm an expert now but I am not!' she said. 'I am just a normal girl in a relationship just like everyone else. No relationship is easier just because you're in the public eye. It's all the same feelings. I am definitely not an expert but what I like to think is that because I have had varied relationships I can be a good listener to the guys and girls and just listen and ask good questions.'

Her relationship with Andrew remained the focus of a huge amount of public attention. Caroline was briefly seen without her engagement ring, sparking frenzied comment, although there was nothing in it, at that moment, at least. Would she and Andrew try for a baby? Friends of both were brought forward to opine. Meanwhile, ratings of *Love Island* soared – not just because of Caroline's own love life, of course, but largely because the nation was becoming increasingly addicted to the goings-on in the famous villa.

But Caroline's love life continued to be tumultuous and, in early July, she announced somewhat tersely that the engagement was off. 'I'm sad to announce that Andrew and I have decided to part ways,' she said. 'Unfortunatel,y it was not to be. I wish him all the best. At least there's a villa waiting for me. It's back to the ol' grafting.'

Andrew also instagrammed: 'Sad to announce Caroline and I have decided to part ways.'

No reasons were given for the split but relations between the two soon turned nasty. Caroline took to Facebook: 'When you find out your fiance had been planning a meeting to go on *Celebs Go Dating* and then has a meeting the day *after* you break up. IN UTTER SHOCK. Kill me now.'

Friends of Andrew said that he was angry to have been made out to be the bad guy in all this while, in the meantime, Caroline was forced to continue her duties on *Love Island*. Andrew then admitted the story was true: 'I never comment on media speculation or stories. But in this instance I feel it necessary to,' he told the *Mirror*. 'Yes, I had a meeting about *Celebs Go Dating* after Caroline and I had separated. However, this was wrong. When someone has no money and nothing to lose they tend to do crazy irrational things. I am ashamed and trying to move on with my life. Please would you respect mine and Caroline's privacy and not try and speculate on who said or did what.'

But public fascination with the couple continued. As Caroline presented *Aftersun*, professional to the last, reports emerged that when the couple had been together they argued constantly. Yet Caroline was still wearing her engagement ring, leading to speculation that they might reunite – after all, they had split up before. Then there were also rumours that Caroline had become close to a crew member on *Love Island*; she did not dignify this with a comment, but posted, 'Life can be bloody hard. People can be bloody mean … but do you know what … keep smiling 'cos Jesus Christ … you have to keep laughing or you'd just cry.'

Andrew was seen taking belongings out of Caroline's flat. There were even rumours they were having arguments about the custody of the dog. There were more cryptic posts from Caroline on Instagram – 'Turn a broken heart into art' – and everything she said about *Love Island* was taken to have a double meaning: of couples in the show, she said, 'But just because some of them haven't lasted, doesn't mean their relationships were a failure. It just means it didn't work out in the long run. Just like a lot of relationships.' Fans wondered, did she have any specific one in mind? There were constant claims – all denied – that Andrew had cheated on her and simply wanted to be with her to raise his profile. Neither of them seemed able to calm matters. Many of these allegations also surfaced just around the time Caroline's loving letter to Andrew appeared in *Cosmopolitan*: the timing could not have been worse.

Love Island came to an end: the winners were Dani Dyer and Jack Fincham. Caroline advised them not to rush their relationship, but they did and subsequently split up. And then there were more dropped jaws when Caroline and Andrew were seen together in Ibiza: it seemed that they had snuck off on a secret break together to see if they could give it another go. 'Caroline can't live with Andrew and she can't live without him,' a friend told the *Sun*. 'The chemistry is incredibly intense, and she really does adore him. But she cannot continue with this rollercoaster of a relationship and is fully aware that something needs to give. After a taking serious heart-to-heart, they gave things one final go. She's taking things day by day.' There were more postings on social media, including a pool picture with a heart emoji captioned, 'An oasis of calm in the middle of crazy.'

That break seemed to have done the trick: the relationship was back on again. And yet, within days, they were seen having a furious argument in a restaurant, Market Café in London Fields, with Andrew overheard by onlookers. It ended with Caroline storming out. 'It's only a small restaurant but, even though they weren't out and out yelling, everyone could hear what they were saying,' a source told the *Sun*. 'You'd think, if they wanted to row they could do it somewhere a bit more private. But things got really intense very quickly. He told her that he thought she was using him so she could get married, but she insisted she loved him and mentioned the Ibiza trip. He was being really argumentative and she said, "You don't need to be so aggressive," and he just kept going until she stormed out, leaving him with the dog. After she left, he just seemed exasperated.'

To those who followed their relationship this was inexplicable: by now there had been numerous break-ups and the two just did not seem able to make a go of it. At the same time, neither did they seem capable of a final break-up. They had only met six months previously, split before they became engaged, became engaged very quickly, split again – no one could understand it. And to make matters worse, it was all carried out very publicly; every row seemed to make the papers. There was one simple explanation, of course – Caroline was really in love and perhaps, having thought she'd met the right man, it was painful to realise he wasn't. But whatever the truth it was clear that they did not have a future together. They just didn't seem able to stay apart.

They took yet another holiday to try to patch things up, this time to St Lucia in the Caribbean. Again the trick worked, briefly: the engagement ring went back on. They were back to attending events together, including the *GQ* Men of the

Year Awards. It was rumoured that they might even already have got married when they were seen sporting gold bands.

And then it all began to go wrong again. There was, of course, another trip, this time in Portugal, to a juice retreat. Here the two had a row, seemingly because Andrew had tried to smuggle alcohol in and had been told off and asked to leave. Off went the engagement ring and on went Caroline to Instagram with another cryptic post: 'People have to pretend you're a bad person so they don't feel guilty about the things they did to you.'

It was against this background that Caroline's thirty-ninth birthday party arrived, a raucous event jointly held with her twin Jody in a private room at a north London pub. Andrew was not there. No explanation was given and great excitement followed about the fact that Caroline had signed up to make a cameo appearance in Steve Coogan's film *Greed*. 'Just wrapped on my first ever film!' Caroline posted, but mention of Andrew was there still none.

Caroline joked about the 'tame' celebrations for her birthday and was soon pictured back at the gym. Andrew did appear still to be on the scene, but their rows grew worse and in November he called an ambulance to Caroline's home. Caroline point-blank denied that this had happened. 'Caroline and Andrew had both been drinking and got into yet another blazing row,' a source told the *Sun*. 'But they weren't even together – they were arguing by phone and it really kicked off between them. Andrew was concerned about her state of mind. At one point she had given the impression she felt like killing herself. Of course, she didn't mean it, but Andrew felt he had no option but to call 999. By the time they arrived, Caroline had sobered up a bit and the crew gave her the once-over. Caroline quickly reassured them that she was OK and didn't pose a risk to herself.' She spent a few days in a London hotel before went filming a *Love Island* Christmas special.

Andrew was later said to have emailed her to apologise for causing the drama and they were shortly afterwards seen together, walking the dog. Her friends didn't know what to make of it all. 'Caroline has been told by so many friends that she should get rid, but she is refusing because she still loves Andrew and is desperate to make it work,' a source told the *Sun On Sunday*. 'Everyone wishes Caroline would realise her worth because she deserves so much better. She could have her pick of any man so it's such a shame she continues to pick him. Andrew never apologises for anything and there is bound to be another fight at some point. They are back together for now and everyone is holding their breath to see what happens next.'

Perhaps unsurprisingly, Caroline became more open about her problems with depression, her use of antidepressants and the undeniable fact that fame didn't provide happiness. Nor did an extremely volatile relationship which, for someone with Caroline's sensitivities and vulnerability, made matters much, much worse. It was dreadfully ironic – her career could not have been soaring any higher and yet there was yet another relationship that had broken down – for the presenter of *Love Island*, at that.

The writing really was on the wall. In December the couple split again, this time for good, just after Caroline made her debut in *Chicago*. 'I'm on my own now,' she confirmed to the *Sun*. 'So, I'm sorting myself out, I'm doing what I want to do. I'm putting my head into this, into work and focusing on acting. We're both looking after our own heads and doing our own thing. That's really important.'

By she refused to condemn Andrew – for now, at least. 'There's two people involved. I don't want to have to bring him up into things when he hasn't got a right to reply. I just really want to get back to me and get back to feeling good again.' Andrew may not have had the right to reply because, as he hinted very strongly the following year, he might have had to sign a non-disclosure agreement.

Caroline, not for the first time, turned to Instagram. She shared her most-liked pictures with her followers, all 1.9 million of them by now, with a rather bittersweet post. 'My top nine … Funny isn't it? I look so happy, except I know in four of those pictures I was dying inside. My top nine moments were not represented by these pictures but by things that happened and will stay in my heart forever. I've learned many lessons this year, mostly that everything is temporary. Moments, feelings, people, flowers, and also having a puppy is bloody hard work. Happy New Year.'

But at least she had *Chicago* and the speed with which she had to learn the role helped too. 'It came at a really good time for me,' she told the *Sun*. 'Literally, the day after we broke up I went into rehearsals and I remember my stylist saying, "Do you know how you're gonna get over this? You're gonna become Roxie. And Roxie's not going through a break-up." And so I became this different person for five weeks. It was an escape from my problems. I woke up as Roxie, went in as Roxie, left as Roxie. It was such a good focus. I remember going on stage on the first night, and … have you ever felt heartbreak where all your skin hurts? I felt like someone had opened my head and poured acid into it and it was going down my body. That's how bad the heartbreak was. But each day on the stage I felt better, I could feel my heart getting stronger, and by the last show I didn't feel that pain any more.'

It was a sad end to what had been a promising beginning, and Andrew had suffered too. He announced he was moving to Australia. 'Dear 2018, you were the biggest lesson in my life. Experiencing the highest highs and the lowest lows with every single emotion and feeling to go with it,' he wrote on Instagram. 'I have learned how much punishment the human mind, heart and body can take, I have felt guilty for things I never even considered someone should feel guilty for and I forgot who I was.'

14

A COMPLEX LIFE

Caroline was a far more complex person than she appeared. Lively, bubbly and energetic on screen, behind the scenes lurked a woman with a depressive streak, prone to massive insecurity. It was the great irony that although she presented a very high-profile dating show and regularly appeared on 'world's sexiest' lists, she had been unable to find happiness within her own personal life.

Despite the break-up with Andrew, 2019 certainly started on a high. *Love Island* loomed, and no one had any idea that Caroline would this year be forced to step down from presenting it. Other projects were flooding in, not least the film *Greed*, in which Caroline had a cameo role. Written by Michael Winterbottom and starring Steve Coogan, David Mitchell and Isla Fisher, it centred on the Roman empire-themed sixtieth birthday party of a character named Sir Richard McCreadie, a retail billionaire, and was a satire on extreme wealth. Caroline was one of a number of celebrities to appear as themselves, others including Stephen Fry, Pixie Lott, Ben Stiller, Colin Firth and Keira Knightley. Caroline was only onscreen for a few moments, introducing Sir

Richard with, 'Now it's time for the man you've all been waiting for, the king of the high street.' By the time the film was released in the UK, in February 2020, Caroline had already died, making it a very poignant moment for many. Steve Coogan paid an emotional tribute to her and called her appearance a 'knockout' in the film.

The film received mixed reviews – reviewers saying that the satire was so heavy-handed that it became almost ineffectual – but a number of the critics picked up on the poignancy of Caroline's last screen appearance. 'The movie is also notable for the final screen appearance of Caroline Flack, who died at the age of forty last week,' wrote Kevin Maher in *The Times*. 'She plays herself at an event that celebrates McCreadie's profits (inflated, natch), his ego and his wife's billion-pound dividend cheque. The scene is supposed to be crass, uncomfortable, and indicative of an especially superficial and ultimately toxic milieu. It has now acquired its own disturbing resonance.'

And Mathew Bond wrote in the *Mail On Sunday*, 'But it's also a film scarred by real-life tragedy, in that the very first shot we see is of the late Caroline Flack, playing herself as the hostess of a tacky, in-house awards ceremony at which Sir Richard will hand out prizes to his overworked employees and vulgarly present his own wife (Isla Fisher) with a dividend cheque for £1.2 billion.'

Jamie East, in the *Sun*, wrote, 'With desperately tragic timing, the first few minutes of the film features what is probably the last screen appearance of Caroline Flack, smiling brightly for the cameras.'

A sombre Steve Coogan went on *BBC Breakfast* to talk about the film after its UK release, and of course, the subject of Caroline came up. 'It was awful. Obviously, my heart goes out to her loved ones and her family,' he said. 'It's tragic. There are lots of issues that are raised by it. I am sure you have talked about that – to do with social media, to do with the press, to do with the discourse that takes place specifically on social media, and also to do with the way the press behave. But I don't particularly want to use what is a tragic death and a tragic occurrence to make political capital out of it. I certainly think that, really, the problem with social media is that people don't see the whites of the eyes of the person they are talking to, so they behave in quite a reprehensible way. You can wax lyrical about it all, but I just think people need to step back and question how they behave, question how they talk to each other. We can disagree with each other but we don't have to be disagreeable.'

Alongside *Greed* in 2019, Caroline had another project in the pipeline, one that was causing a great deal of controversy. The premise of *The Surjury* was that young people who wanted to have cosmetic surgery would make their case before a jury. In order to get the work approved, they would have to get 75 per cent of the jury voting for them for procedures that included bum lifts, sculpted abs and breast enlargements. The makers of the programme, Gobstopper Television, were understandably keen to talk it up. 'This is a totally new way of doing peer-to-peer advice,' said executive producer Ross McCarthy. 'Our pitchers will either get the surgery they've always wanted, or a massive boost in confidence when the public rules they don't need work at all.'

'*The Surjury* is an innovative format that promises to literally get under the skin of people who think that a quick fix is their best option,' said Becky Cadman, Channel 4's factual entertainment commissioning editor.

Channel 4 itself also chimed in with a statement. '*The Surjury* allows people to explore their choices more thoroughly and to take measured advice from their peers, some of whom may previously have gone under the knife themselves and will happily hold court on the subject.'

The broadcaster's CEO, Alex Mahon said, 'This is not intended to be exploitative and tawdry but is bringing to the fore an important issue in society today. There are huge volumes of cosmetic surgery in society and there have been shows dealing with cosmetic surgery for decades, such as *Extreme Makeover*. The question is, can we create a useful discussion about what that means in society and whether the current rates of cosmetic surgery are acceptable?'

Not surprisingly, however, given the nature of the programme, there was immediate uproar, not least from plastic surgeons themselves. 'We are extremely concerned about the message this programme portrays and its particular focus on young people,' said surgeon Mark Henley, president of the British Association of Plastic, Reconstructive and Aesthetic Surgeons (BAPRAS). 'Based on the promotional materials alone, we believe the show will trivialise the serious decision all should take when considering aesthetic procedures. It is disappointing that, in 2019, we are still having to remind large broadcasters of the potential harm caused by glamorising cosmetic surgery – particularly when targeting young adults or those with self-esteem issues.'

Although he certainly wasn't alone in expressing concern, the show went ahead, with Caroline announced as the presenter. Caroline herself had been open about her insecurities with her own body and in an interview about *Love Island*, the subject of plastic surgery came up. 'It's a funny one, and I'm not going to slag it off because I'm not saying that I'd never have anything done in the future,' she told the *Sun*. 'I may or may not have. I can't confirm or deny. You do little things here and there to make yourself feel a bit better, but there is a side to it where people go too far. There's no way you should be able to walk into surgery with lips the size of a lilo and be able to go any bigger. It's dangerous and sends the wrong message to young girls. You can just literally be born with one face now and die with a different one.'

As the casting call for *The Surjury* went out in August, Caroline was in good spirits. She posted a picture of herself with a glass of bubbly, appearing to be totally naked apart from a strategically placed champagne bottle: 'Over the moooooon to be hosting my first Channel 4 show, *The Surjury*.'

Ross McCarthy said, 'Caroline is the perfect safe pair of hands for a format that taps into the social phenomenon of elective surgery.'

Becky Cadman was equally pleased to welcome her. 'We're delighted to have Caroline on board,' she said of Channel 4's approach to plastic surgery. 'With Caroline and the jury's help, this new series looks at who wants it and why, allowing those who make a strong enough case to their peers, to undergo the procedure of their choice. The show will neither glamorise nor condemn their choices: the aim is instead to interrogate the realities.'

Caroline was pictured all over London, partying hard. But criticism of the show did not die down: a number of newspaper columnists condemned it, while presenter Jameela Jamil weighed into the debate on social media with a reference to Charlie Brooker's dystopian satire. '*Black Mirror* is officially happening guys. It's here,' she wrote.

'Have you managed to see a copy before me?' Caroline replied. 'Please forward … am desperate to see.'

This was not an end to the online debate: other social media users piled in to have their say, with the usual arguing. Caroline engaged, as she always did, when it would have been far better just to walk away. The typical pile-on began and it was known that Caroline would obsessively read absolutely everything as it came up. She defended her new show. 'I've filmed it and the people who have taken part are amazing and have been through a lot and life is about individual choice,' she told one poster.

Whatever the merits of the programme, this response was still quite a new phenomenon. Television presenters had not had to face such a daily onslaught from the public before social media. Criticism and reviews in the national press, yes, but not the kind of engagement that made her feel as if she was under personal attack.

'After reading about your personal journey with your mental health I'm surprised at your choice of job but ultimately they would have got another presenter,' said one.

'Well, mental health is a sensitive subject and as we progress we are constantly asked to be more open and visible,' Caroline replied. 'My feeling toward the show is that it opens up conversations on why some people turn to surgery to help them lead the life that they believe will make them happier.'

As the furore raged, others in the TV industry stepped in to speak up for the programme again. Becky Cadman issued a press release: 'All contributors featured in the series have actively been seeking surgery of their own accord. The show will neither glamorise nor condemn their choices: the aim is instead to interrogate the realities.'

As surgeons went public on why they would not choose to take part in such a show, Channel 4 issued a press release: 'Cosmetic surgery has become an increasingly mainstream choice in Britain. *The Surjury* seeks to explore why so many people feel the need to change their bodies, and whether surgery actually makes them happier ... this new series allows them to consult with surgical teams and then to discuss their reasons for wanting it with a panel of their peers. If their peers support their decision they will undergo the procedure of their choice subject to the usual surgical checks and consent processes ... duty of care to contributors is of paramount importance and all will be independently assessed by the clinic who will carry out their procedure. They will be psychologically assessed and supported regarding their involvement in the programme.'

The 'duty of care' issue was an increasingly important one, and it had cropped up in the context of other reality shows, specifically *Love Island* and Jeremy Kyle's show. A spate of suicides had been linked to both programmes: *Love Island*'s Sophie Gradon had taken her own life in 2018, while contestant Mike Thalassitis did the same in 2019. Meanwhile, a Kyle guest had been found dead at home, some days after having failed a lie detector test when trying to convince his partner that he was faithful.

All three deaths had shocked not just the makers of the shows, but also the public. And it was estimated that since 1986, thirty-eight participants in reality TV shows had taken their own lives. With the advent of social media, the problem had become far more acute: 'The bosses are so worried about offending anybody they're allowing people with histories of eating disorders, mental health problems, anxiety and depression to take part,' a reality TV source told the Sun. 'People are going on these shows who aren't strong enough to cope. They come out to millions of social media followers, trolls, hangers-on. Some are national hate figures. For a young person with a mental health condition, it's a lethal combination.'

Less controversially, Caroline made an appearance on *The Great Celebrity Bake Off*, in aid of Stand Up To Cancer. She was shown alongside Channel 4 newsreader Krishnan Guru-Murthy, actor Greg Wise and boxer Nicola Adams and the four were asked to make a 3D selfie using twenty-four biscuits. Caroline's effort featured a green wire nose and pink candyfloss hair: 'That's one of the weirdest things I've ever seen, let alone made,' she confessed.

While all this was going on, interest remained as strong as ever in Caroline's own personal life. Recently returned from a holiday in Dubai with her friend, the actor, dancer and former singer with The Pussycat Dolls, Ashley Roberts, there was great excitement when she was spotted with rugby player Danny Cipriani (who had also dated Kelly Brooks and Sophie Gradon), although this was never much more than a fling. 'He's obviously very into her, and to be fair they make a great-looking couple,' a source told the *Sun*. 'They did start tongues wagging quite quickly. Of course, he does have a reputation as a lothario, but Caroline is clearly a confident woman who seems to be able to handle herself. If anything it looked as though she was calling the shots and he was a bit infatuated. But they were around for a few days so things are obviously going pretty well.'

The couple were seen together a few more times, with various of Danny's exes queuing up to warn Caroline that it would not work. She was reportedly upset when Kelly Brook, Danny's most famous ex, weighed in. 'I can't believe she's doing *Love Island* and dating Danny Cipriani,' Kelly said on Heart radio. 'I was, like, "Is she just following my life or something?" Hang on, I was the first host of *Love Island*, then I dated Danny. It's like, what's next? Is she going to come and start hosting this show next? I don't know if she's still dating him. But when I look at stuff like that I'm, like, "This is just weird. It's just weird."'

It wasn't that weird: they all moved in the same circles. But nor did the relationship last and Caroline then revealed that she had joined the Raya dating app, designed for people in the public eye. In the end, she met her last great love, tennis player Lewis Burton, the old fashioned way – in person that August.

As with so many of her boyfriends, Lewis was younger than her, born on 23 March 1992, and twenty-seven when their relationship began. Born in the Bexley area of London, he started playing tennis at the age of seven and played the finals of the boys' doubles at Wimbledon in 2010. He was also a model, on the books of Select Model Management. The relationship went public when Lewis put a picture of the two of them on Instagram (naturally) with Caroline kissing him on the cheek. It was captioned, 'Self-confessed Caroline Flack.' Lewis was shirtless, Caroline was in a frilly black bikini.

They certainly seemed pretty happy, too. 'Caroline and Lewis were introduced through mutual friends and have really hit it off,' a source told the *Sun*. 'They've been on several dates now and are getting on really well. Lewis has been a true gent to Caroline and has patiently waited to see her. She has been jetting back and forth between London and Majorca as she juggles her presenting commitments, but they have been spending time together when they can. They feel comfortable in each other's company and it seems to be going in the right direction.'

In no time the pair were going strong. They were seen out and about on the celebrity circle, attending the *Love Island* wrap party, out at the theatre (*Waitress*, featuring Ashley Roberts) and all appeared to be on track. But Caroline was nearing forty now and she was clearly ruminating on her life and the fact that she had not yet had children and settled down.

'I've kind of always put work first,' she told Kathy Burke on Channel 4's *All Woman*. 'Wake up in the morning, go to work, come home – just like my boyfriend has. I'm scared it's going to get too late; where I've wanted to go, "Right, maybe slow down, think about having kids and maybe think about settling down," but I've never had that. I feel guilty for it sometimes, I feel like maybe I'm being selfish.' And, of course, there was the ongoing interest in her love life. 'Being single shouldn't be seen as a sign of weakness. When you're on your own, you're more powerful because you're not relying on someone else. So it's actually more of a powerful thing to be single. And when you're single and happy, that is when you feel at your best.'

Despite that, Caroline and Lewis continued to be seen out, attending The Big Feastival together. On the subject of food, Caroline again discussed her love of gravy: 'I'm not addicted to a lot of things, like I don't drink a lot of coffee and I don't have an addictive personality,' she told Mo Gilligan on Channel 4's *The Lateish Show*. 'But I religiously like to eat roast dinners. Now you can't have a roast dinner every day, can you? So sometimes I just have a cup of gravy. I just like Bisto. In fact, they sent me a range with my name on the pack. I take my own gravy to dinners. My sister makes terrible gravy so I always turn up with my own gravy. Sorry, Jo. She knows.' In other words, all seemed to be normal and well.

She and Lewis holidayed in Ibiza, where they were seen on a yacht with friends. But for the first time there were signs of trouble: the pair appeared to be arguing, with Caroline waving her hands in the air and, on occasion, seeming tearful. The next day the pair appeared to be loved up again, but there were still hints of problems behind the scenes. This was borne out once she was back in London and took, again, to Instagram: 'Back from holiday … Not quite as relaxing as I thought but ready to jump back into work! NEWWWWW JOB THIS WEEK … all to be revealed soon.' This was *The Surjury*, the show that would never ultimately be seen.

Did it help that Caroline put so very much of her life on screen? In one way her openness was commendable, but she shared so much that it made her more vulnerable than she might otherwise have been. If every last aspect of her life was there for anyone to comment on, it was bound to have an effect on her when the trolls got going. And given that she had had such a public and bruising split a short time earlier, was it really wise to leave herself open to this again?

But sharing online had become a way of life for Caroline. She read all the comments, engaged with anonymous keyboard warriors and took everything that was said to heart. Trolling was something that everyone in the public eye had to put up with, especially women, but Caroline didn't see that the best response was to ignore it. She didn't seem able to do so.

The couple seemed back on track, but Caroline took to Instagram again, now to discuss the issue of mental health. In retrospect, it is easy to see that she was in a far more fragile state than anyone realised, and that the disastrous events about to engulf her were just too much to cope with, but at the time it merely seemed that she was being open about a subject that many people simply didn't want to address. Was this a cry for help – possibly a subconscious one? Probably even Caroline herself didn't know.

'I wanted to write something about [World] Mental Health Day last week but I was knee-deep in work,' she began. 'And some days it's hard to write your feelings if you're not in the right place. The last few weeks I've been in a really weird place … I find it hard to talk about it … I guess it's anxiety and pressure of life … and when I actually reached out to someone they said I was draining. I feel like this is why some people keep their emotions to themselves. I certainly hate talking about my feelings. And being a burden is my biggest fear … I'm lucky to be able to pick myself up when things feel s**t. But what happens if someone can't? Be nice to people. You never know what's going on. Ever.'

It didn't help that the controversy about *The Surjury* was still going strong. In the past, when Caroline's private life had been rocky, at least she still had work to fall back on, but now that side of her life was under attack too. And, while she was widely praised for being so open about mental health issues, there was still clearly no real understanding, among the public at least, of what she was going through. Caroline's family and friends knew that her confident, glamorous image was not at all the full story, but to everyone else she still appeared to be a golden girl with the world at her feet.

And, in part, Caroline's own actions added to this view of her life. She posted a picture of herself lying topless in bed in a pair of white jeans, her modesty preserved by a book. It prompted a host of appreciative comments, as it was meant to. And she still had a sense of humour – the image was captioned, 'I was young and I needed the money.' And her relationship with Lewis seemed to be back on track, too. There were rumours of an engagement– strongly denied – but the two seemed happy to be out and about with each other. Lewis organised a surprise party for Caroline's fortieth birthday at the Bagatelle restaurant in London; it went on until well into the early hours and guests included Caroline's co-celebrating twin Jody. It was a truly happy occasion, with many friends and family members in attendance.

And, of course, she took to Instagram. 'Last day of my thirties ... and what a ride it's been so far ... feeling so utterly grateful for *everything* in my life right now ... and never felt quite so happy as I do today ... Can't *wait* for this weekend ... and forty isn't old ... if you're a tree.'

15

FINALE

Fans were stunned when Caroline Flack was arrested and charged with assault just before Christmas of 2019. Six police cars were called to the scene and it soon emerged that the man Caroline had been charged with assaulting was Lewis, who was by then sharing her home. He had been taken to hospital but his injuries were 'not serious' and he soon went home.

'Caroline Flack, forty, of Islington was charged on Friday 13 December with assault by beating,' said a Metropolitan police spokesperson. 'She will appear on bail at Highbury Corner magistrates' court on Monday 23 December. This follows an incident at approximately 5.25 a.m. on Thursday 12 December after reports of a man being assaulted. He was not seriously injured.'

An Ambulance Service spokesman said, 'We were called yesterday, Thursday 12 December, at 5.28 a.m. to a residential address in Islington. We treated two people at the scene and took one person to hospital.'

The timing could not have been worse. This was just a couple of weeks before Caroline was due to fly out to South

Africa to film *Love Island*'s winter series, a move that was immediately put in doubt. She went uncharacteristically quiet on social media, while Lewis made it immediately apparent that he did not want to press charges. 'Lewis is very upset and embarrassed about how this situation has blown up,' a friend told Mailonline. 'It was a tiff between a couple that love each other and should never have ended up in the public domain … he has not and is not pressing charges. He loves Caroline and wants things to be back to normal as soon as possible.'

It was a wish that was not to be granted. Pictures emerged of a blood-spattered front door. Yet a friend of Caroline's reported that the couple were indeed still very much together, with Lewis posting a picture of the two of them alongside a red heart emoji, but it very quickly emerged that the drama was not going to blow over. *Love Island* bosses were holding crisis talks about what to do; it was said that Caroline was terrified her television career was over.

Caroline's flat had been up for sale since the previous September and there was now the added interest of the home being the site of the alleged assault. Andrew Brady posted a picture of a non-disclosure agreement (NDA), but with names redacted, prompting Lewis to speak out: 'I'm tired of the lies and abuse aimed at my girlfriend,' he said. 'This is not a witch-hunt – this is someone's life. I have not signed any NDA. Why would I? Caroline is the most lovely girl. Loyal and kind. She doesn't deserve any of this.'

She didn't but it didn't stop the coverage. Social media went into overdrive – naturally – and a few days later Caroline herself announced that she was stepping back from *Love Island*. She issued a statement: 'There have been a significant number of media reports and allegations in regard to my personal life. While matters were not as have been reported, I am committed to co-operating with the appropriate authorities and I can't comment further on these matters until the legal process is over. However, *Love Island* has been my world for the last five years, it's the best show on telly. In order to not detract attention from the upcoming series I feel the best thing I can do is to stand down for series six. I want to wish the incredible team working on the show a fantastic series in Cape Town.'

She was to be replaced by the Irish presenter and actress Laura Whitmore, girlfriend of narrator Iain Stirling. Caroline could not have been nicer: 'I'm glad it's Laura,' she instagrammed. 'She loves the show as much as I do.' It was thought that Caroline might be absent for just the one series.

More gruesome details of the alleged assault were to occur. In court on 23 December, Caroline pleaded not guilty. Prosecutor Kate Weiss said, 'At 5.25 a.m. on 12 December he [Lewis Burton] made an allegation against his girlfriend Caroline Flack. Police then made their way to the address. Police then knocked on the door eight minutes later and it was opened by both of them. Both were covered in blood. And, in fact, one of the police officers likened the scene to a horror movie. He (Burton) said he had been asleep and had been hit over the head by Caroline by a lamp. It cut his head and his face was covered in blood.

'He said that Caroline smashed a glass and caused injuries. She had two lacerations to her left wrist. She took his phone while he was sleeping. She had seen text messages which made her think he was cheating. In the 999 call the complainant said quite clearly that his girlfriend was beating him up. He asked repeatedly for help. He was almost begging the operator to send help. He said: "She is going mad, breaking stuff. I've just woken up. She's cracked my head open." The defendant is calling him an a***hole saying, "It's all your fault, you've ruined my life," calling him an a***hole repeatedly. He said, "You've cracked my head open." He told the operator, "She tried to kill me, mate."' Caroline was also said to have gone berserk in police custody, flipping over a table and having to be 'restrained on the ground'.

But – and it was a big but – Lewis did not support the prosecution. He was insistent that he was not a victim and Caroline's lawyer, Paul Morris, told the court that they were still a couple. Caroline was clearly in a terrible state; sobbing in court, having posted on Instagram the night before, 'This is the worst time of my life. I don't know where to go. Where to look. Who to trust. Or even who I am.'

Lewis was not allowed to see Caroline (perhaps if he had been the outcome would have been different), but he did what he could. He came to the court to support her and denied point-blank that she had hit him with a lamp. 'It's heartbreaking I can't see my girlfriend over Christmas,' he said. 'What I witnessed today was horrible. She did not hit me with a lamp. Arguments do happen every day in every relationship. Gutted I am not allowed to protect her right now.'

Caroline took to Instagram again. 'Thankfully I know a lot of you will not believe all that you have heard and read following today's court hearing … thank you for your continued support and love … It's going to be a relief when I am able to give my side of the story, when I'm allowed to.' She was released on bail and a trial date was set for 4 March. She was hugged by her mother as the family left.

The question remains to this day: why, since Lewis had no desire to press charges, did the case go ahead? It was at the behest of the Crown Prosecution Service, who came in for a good deal of criticism in the wake of Caroline's death, although in fairness, no one had any idea of the tragedy that was looming. In many domestic abuse cases – the vast majority of which have a female victim – the complaint is withdrawn. This may well be because the abuser is still in contact with and has influence over their victim and has put pressure on them to do so and for this reason the CPS is reluctant to step back once a proceeding has begun. The CPS was not to blame any more than anyone else in this tragedy (with the exception of social media trolls) but it was certainly unfortunate that, despite the fact that Caroline and Lewis were still a couple and wanted to be together, the case was set to go ahead.

Caroline's defence asked to remove bail conditions that prevented her from contacting Lewis and from attending his address, but this was refused by district judge Julia Newton. 'They had been in a relationship all of this year and he appears in court today to support her and they remain a couple,' said Paul Morris. 'She wants to spend time with her partner. If the conditions were lifted there would be no concerns. It's not an irrelevant point, it's Christmas, it's new year, she's suffered enough.' It was not to be.

Friends were now actively urging Caroline to stay away from social media, but it seems she could not. She went to Instagram, sharing an old picture of herself on the red carpet: 'Been advised not to go on social media … but I wanted to say Happy Christmas to everyone who has been so incredibly kind to me this year,' she said. 'This kind of scrutiny and speculation is a lot to take on for one person to take on their own … I'm a human being at the end of the day and I'm not going to be silenced when I have a story to tell and a life to keep going with … I'm taking some time out to get feeling better and learn some lessons from situations I've got myself into to. I have nothing but love to give and best wishes for everyone.'

Social media lived down to expectations. Someone managed to find an old tweet that Caroline had sent when she bought a new lamp: 'I like my new lamp.'

'That didn't age very well,' tweeted someone else of the nine-year-old post and, trivial as that might sound to most people, as we now know, Caroline was in a very bad way. Others were making lamp-related jokes at her expense, too, and it was causing a great deal more anguish than anyone saw. *The Surjury* was also under threat, with doubts over whether it would ever broadcast.

Caroline spent Christmas with friends and volunteering at Golden Years, a charity in Hackney that hosted Christmas lunches for socially isolated older people. She headed for a break in LA to get away from it all but then pictures emerged of Caroline's bedroom with blood on the sheets. Lewis again attempted to calm matters: taking to Instagram he said, 'Bullshit: this blood isn't mine and I didn't get hit over the head with a lamp, can everyone stop now?' He then posted a photo of him and Caroline having a drink: 'I love this girl more than anything, no one knows what's going on or what's happened. She's fucking harmless and the most amazing person I have ever met.' Indeed, it appeared that the blood was actually Caroline's but the scene was so dramatically gory that it merely set off fresh waves of speculation and alarm.

Love Island kicked off on 12 January, with Laura praising Caroline. 'She has been incredibly gracious and supportive of me taking on the role for the winter series', she said. 'She's a brilliant host and I just hope that I can give the role the justice it deserves while she is taking some time off.' But it can't have helped Caroline's state of mind that she was edited out of the *Love Island* trailer: she was to have been shown wandering through a group of singletons. ITV was quick to react – they were in 'constant contact' with Caroline, they said, and the door was open for her at any time.

Caroline had not been on social media anything like as much as usual, but she returned as the show launched: 'Massive good luck to Laura, Iain and the team for tonight's launch show ... the first one always the best one. Caroline x'.

In fact, ratings dropped and there was some concern that the programme should air only once a year. Caroline, meanwhile, returned to the UK towards the end of the month, looking fit and healthy, having apparently not had a drink since before Christmas and having followed an intensive gym routine. There were reassuring noises from both ITV and Channel 4 about wanting to work with her again, but everyone seemed to accept that she had to get through the court case first. There were also reports that she wanted to change her lifestyle, ditch the party-girl image, drop alcohol and make a fresh start.

But there were other concerns. Caroline's flat had been on the market: now she took it off and rented it out instead – she had lost her £1.2 million *Love Island* salary. At The National Television Awards, Caroline was absent, but was the subject of an unkind dig by host David Walliams. *The Masked Singer* presenter Joel Dommett came on with a hedgehog-costumed character: 'Thank you Joel and so nice to see Caroline Flack back on TV as well,' he said. This was met with boos.

Caroline returned to social media: 'I'm going to speak today .. mine and my family's life is no longer up for entertainment or gossip.' But nothing more was forthcoming, possibly on legal advice. There were yet more stories that she and Lewis had split, strongly denied by the man himself. Friends were getting worried; one spoke out to say that Caroline was not in a good place. There were fears her career was over and that she wasn't sleeping. The poor woman was clearly getting into a dreadful state. She was said to fear being judged by the public – although, if anything, she had quite a lot of support.

But she still read social media, the place where anyone in the public eye can be guaranteed to find negativity. And find it she did. Even so there were rumours that she was penning a self-help book. It was not to be.

On 13 February Caroline was pictured on a climbing wall with her friend, TV producer Mollie Grosberg, posted on the latter's Instagram feed, prompting an affectionate post from Lewis, 'You're both useless.' The comment was later taken down as the two were not supposed to be in touch, but the reality is that they were communicating as much by social media as was possible. Denying split rumours, Lewis also posted a picture of the two of them together: 'We ain't split,' it said with a red heart, while underneath was the message, 'Can't wait to see you.' On 14 February, Lewis posted a picture of the two of them with the caption, 'Happy Valentine's. Love you' and a kissing-face emoji. Caroline posted a picture of herself, with her dog Ruby. It was to be her last post. On 15 February, the shocking news emerged that Caroline had died. Later, her family confirmed that it was by her own hand.

The flood of shock and grief was overwhelming. No one had realised that things had got so bad. Tributes began pouring in, from her old friend Keith Lemon, from Ant and Dec, from Laura Whitmore, from various *Love Island* stars. Zoe Ball and Philip Schofield both paid tribute. There was a sense of disbelief. People began apportioning blame. Some called for *Love Island* to be taken off the air (this was the third suicide associated with the show). Boy George accused the CPS of heartlessness, along with everyone else who had called for the trial to go ahead. Various footballers, themselves sometimes victims of trolling, called for people to be kinder on social media.

ITV released a statement expressing shock and, in fact, so did many others associated with Caroline, including the *Love Island* production company, her old stage school and people who merely had seen her on television and commented on how relatable she was. Friends posted previously unseen pictures of her. There was a sense, not just of grief but of guilt. How could this effervescent woman who still had a life before her have done something so drastic? But Caroline had suffered from depression; everyone knew that.

A devastated Lewis spoke out. 'My heart is broken. We had something so special. I am so lost for words, I am in so much pain; I miss you so much. I know you felt safe with me, you always said I don't think about anything else when I am with you and I was not allowed to be there this time. I kept asking and asking.' He vowed to find out why they had not been allowed to see one another: 'I will be your voice, baby, I promise I will ask all the questions you wanted and I will get all the answers. Nothing will bring you back but I will try make you proud every day. I love you with all my heart.'

Caroline's management company was in no doubt who was to blame. 'The CPS pursued this when they knew not only how very vulnerable Caroline was but also that the alleged victim did not support the prosecution and had disputed the CPS version of events,' they said in a statement.

'The CPS should look at themselves today and how they pursued a show trial that was not only without merit but not in the public interest. And ultimately resulted in significant distress to Caroline.'

Others lashed out in fury at an industry that had appeared to let Caroline down (it had been noted that when Ant McPartlin went through a particularly difficult period in his personal life and was forced to take a break from *I'm A Celebrity*, TV bosses had been extremely supportive).

Amanda Holden took to Instagram: 'For Caroline to feel that death was the only way out breaks my heart. Anger doesn't even begin to cover how I feel about her being thrown to the dogs like she was. Why was she not shown the same level of consideration, protection, warmth and importance as other artists in our industry who have struggled recently? I am certain there is more to her story ... I know the truth will out. May she rest in peace and those responsible for this lack of humanity be brave enough to admit their shame.'

Olly Murs, unsurprisingly, was devastated and had not 'stopped crying'. 'I remember messaging you at your toughest time to let you know that I never read or listened to any of the crap people were saying,' he said.

Love Island went off air for one night in tribute, although there was some disquiet that the participants had no idea what had happened and were carrying on much as before. There were also calls for it to be taken off air permanently, although it seemed highly unlikely that was ever going to happen. Danny Cipriani revealed his devastation at missing a call from her because he'd been playing rugby.

There was more. It was said that Caroline feared that bodycam footage would be made public and thus ruin her career forever; 'I hear that the footage is quite distressing,' said a friend. It was also said that she told the police she would commit suicide. Andrew Brady lashed out angrily at Caroline's management and PR people and expressed his own love for the star.

In the middle of it all was her devastated family, who released the Instagram post detailed at the beginning of this book. 'Carrie sent me this message at the end of January but was told not to post it by advisers but she so wanted to have her little voice heard,' her mother Chris said. 'So many untruths were out there but this is how she felt and my family and I would like people to read her own words. Carrie was surrounded by love and friends but this was just too much for her. Her friends Molly, Lou, Sam, Liam and Simon need a very special mention and lots of thanks for trying so hard to keep her safe. Jody her twin sister was there her whole life for her, but this time nothing could take away the hurt of such injustice.

Caroline's funeral was held on 10 March, in a private ceremony for family and friends. It took place in Norfolk, Caroline's home, and her mother Chris later described it to the *Eastern Daily Press*: the two-hour service at GreenAcres Colney had 'lots of memories, smiles but mostly tears'. She thanked people who had 'travelled from all over the world'. 'Friends included all the old pals she had either worked alongside or presented with on *Fash FC*, *I'm A Celebrity*, *Xtra Factor*, *Love Island*; friends old and new from the world of *Strictly*, the *Bake Off* and many, many more. Her friends from school days, college days and present day also gathered to exchange stories and pay tributes to my beautiful girl.'

No pictures were released, but the ceremony was known to have taken place in a woodland hall filled with flowers. *X Factor* contestant Lucie Jones performed a song from *Waitress*.

What will the legacy of Caroline Flack be? She will, of course, be remembered as a brilliant and bubbly television presenter who pursued a glittering career. Yet beyond that, perhaps her story might also make people think twice before posting on social media. The last word should be Caroline's: 'In a world where you can be anything – be kind.'